Teach Yourself
SPANISH

Published by
Lotus Press Publishers & Distributors

TEACH YOURSELF
SPANISH

Sonya Surabhi Gupta
Nabiel Ansari

4735/22, Prakash Deep Building,
Ansari Road, Daryaganj,
New Delhi - 110002

Lotus Press : Publishers & Distributors
Unit No. 220, 2nd Floor, 4735/22, Prakash Deep Building,
Ansari Road, Darya Ganj, New Delhi- 110002
Ph.: 41325510, 98118-38000
• E-mail : lotuspress1984@gmail.com
www.lotuspress.co.in

Teach Yourself Spanish

ISBN: 978-81-8382-309-8

Printed & Published by : **Lotus Press Publishers & Distributors,** New Delhi-02

PREFACE

This book is aimed at providing beginners with a tool for learning Spanish on their own. It will equip learners with a functional knowledge of Spanish in order to use it in various contexts. Spanish is a widely spoken language with about 350 million native speakers spread across more than 20 countries. It is also the second language of the USA and a fair amount of global business involves the Spanish-speaking world.

The book uses insights of the communicative approach representative of real life communication. The learners will be introduced to the structures and usage of Spanish. They will carry out communicative activities and also learn the active grammar and vocabulary needed to carry them out.

It is hoped that through this book, learners will be able to:

- Understand simple texts/conversations in Spanish;
- Understand and participate in simple conversations in the situations dealt with in the book
- Read and comprehend simple texts
- Write brief texts, be able to write their Curriculum Vitae, etc
- Have some familiarity with the socio-cultural diversity of the Spanish-speaking world

This book has fifteen lessons covering various communicative contexts. Each lesson has dialogues, vocabulary, grammar, tasks and exercises and a note on some cultural aspect of the Spanish speaking world. At the end of the book we have also appended an Additional vocabulary as well as the key which offers solutions to the exercises given in each lesson. The CD will help the learners in mastering the pronunciation as well as developing the skills of listening comprehension.

We hope that this book will be useful to those who need to use Spanish in their professional environment.

The authors would like to thank Shweta Sahay for her suggestions and valuable inputs as well as the support in the course of the preparation of this book.

Authors

CONTENTS

CHAPTER

Spanish is not difficult

See the following pictures and make out the meaning of the words given against them

Aeropuerto	Metro

Teléfono	Diccionario español- inglés

Restaurante	

Surely this was not difficult! To start with, the easier part of learning Spanish on your own is that you don't have to struggle with a new script. But as you must have already noticed there are some new alphabets (for example **ñ** in *español* which means Spanish) and some new signs (for example **é** in ingl**é**s, which means English). Moreover, Spanish alphabets are pronounced differently even though they seem the same as English.

Task: Make a list of words and expressions that you already know in Spanish, from books and comics, from films, from music.

THE SPANISH ALPHABET/ EL ABECEDARIO ESPAÑOL

According to the Real Academia Española [The Royal Academy of Spain], the Spanish alphabet, like other romance languages, is based on the Latin alphabet and adapted throughout the centuries to what it is today. The Spanish alphabet is formed of twenty-seven letters:

Alphabet name	Alphabet	Pronunciation	Examples
a	**A,a**	Like the "**a**" in "f**a**ther"	M**a**cho
be	**B,b**	Like the "**b**" in "**b**ank"	**B**anco, Cu**b**a
ce	**C,c**	Like the "**c**" in "**c**ar" when before "a", "o" or "u" or a consonant	**C**armen, **C**ola, **C**uba, **C**rema
		Like the "**c**" in "**c**ell" when it comes before "e" or "i"	**C**entro Bar**c**elona, **C**ine
che	**Ch,ch**	Like the "**ch**" in "**ch**ur**ch**"	**Ch**ile, ma**cho**
de	**D,d**	Like "**th**" in "**th**at"	**D**inero, Na**d**al
e	**E,e**	Like the "**e**" in "b**e**t"	**E**nrique, Rafa**e**l
efe	**F,f**	Like the "**f**" in "**f**or"	**F**ernando, **f**iesta

ge	**G,g**	Like the "g" in "go" when it comes before "a", "o" or "u" or a consonant	**Ga**s, **Go**lfo, **Gu**sto, I**gl**esia, **Gr**acias
		When it comes before "e" or "i", it is a strongly aspirated "h" and pronounced something like "kh"	**Ge**nte, **Gi**mnasia Ar**ge**ntina
hache	**H,h**	It is silent and not pronounced at all	**H**otel, **H**ola, A**h**ora
i	**I,i**	Like "ee" in "meet", though shorter	Enr**i**que **I**gles**i**as,
jota	**J,j**	It is like a strongly aspirated "h", and is pronounced something like "kh" (it has the same sound what "g" has when before "e" or "i")	**J**ardín, A**j**o, **J**uan
ca	**K,k**	It is found only in foreign words and pronounced like "k" in "kilo"	**Kilómetro**
ele	**L,l**	Like "l" in "lake"	**L**atino, **L**orca
elle	**Ll,ll**	Like 'll" in "million" in Spain and the "y" in "yellow" in Latin America	Ca**ll**e, **Ll**amar
eme	**M,m**	Like "m" in "mother"	**M**adre, **M**ercosur
ene	**N,n**	Like "n" in "nose"	**N**acho**s**, **N**eruda
eñe	**Ñ,ñ**	Like"ny" in "Sonya" or "canyon"	Espa**ñ**a, Ni**ñ**o
o	**O,o**	Like "o" in "cone", though shorter	Comerci**o**, **O**j**o**

pe	**P,p**	Like "p" in "speak"	**P**laza, Es**p**añol
cu	**Q,q**	Like "k", It comes with "u" which is not pronounced	Már**qu**ez, **Qu**ito
ere	**R,r**	Like "r" in "rice" but rolled on the tip of the tongue more than in English , even more rolled when "r" comes initially	Fe**r**nando To**rr**es **R**afael
ese	**S,s**	Like "s" in "sin", not like "z" ever	**S**opa, E**s**pañol,
te	**T,t**	The "t" is pronounced soft in Spanish, unlike in English	**T**urismo, pa**t**a**t**a
u	**U,u**	Like "oo" in "root"	**U**nión E**u**ropea
uve	**V,v**	Pronounced exactly like "b" in Spanish. Both "b" and "v" are pronounced like "b" in "bank"	**V**ino, **V**illa
uve doble	**W,w**	It is found only in foreign words and pronounced as "w" in "water"	**W**hisky, **W**ashington
equis	**X,x**	It varies in sound depending on the origin of the word. Generally pronounced as "x" as in "exile"	E**x**amen
i griega	**Y,y**	Like "y" in "yes". But alone or at the end of the word it is like the vowel "i"	**Y**ate, **Y**olanda So**y**, Re**y**

zeta	Z,z	Like "s" in "sin, not like "z" ever, though sometimes it is voiced	**Z**apato, **Z**orro

This variation of the Latin alphabet has been used since 1803. Since this date, **ch** and **ll** have been in the alphabet to represent themselves with individual sounds. However, in 1994 it was decided that words beginning with **ch** and **ll** should be alphabetized in the same place as the letters **c** and **l** respectively. This reform only affects the process in which the words are alphabetized and not the composition of the alphabet.

REMEMBER:

ca, co ,cu, que, qui sound as: [k] (like "c" in "car")	In most of Spain and Latin America za, zo, zu, ce, ci sound as : [s] (like "s" in "sin") In Castillian Spanish, considered standard Spanish by many, it is [θ] (like a lisping of "th")
ja, jo, ju, je, ji, ge, gi sound as : [x] like strongly aspirated "h" or "kh"	
ga, go, gu, gue, gui sound as : [g]	
b and v sound the same as: [b]	
h is not pronounced at all	

VOCABULARY

The Numbers

0 cero	8 ocho
1 uno	9 nueve
2 dos	10 diez
3 tres	11 once
4 cuatro	12 doce
5 cinco	13 trece
6 seis	14 catorce
7 siete	15 quince

16 dieciséis	70 setenta
17 diecisiete	80 ochenta
18 dieciocho	90 noventa
19 diecinueve	100 cien
20 veinte	101 ciento uno
21 veintiuno	200 doscient**os/as**
22 veintidós	240 doscient**os/as** cuarenta
23 veintitrés	300 trescient**os/as**
24 veinticuatro	400 cuatrocient**os/as**
25 veinticinco	600 seiscient**os/as**
26 veintiséis	700 setecient**os/as**
27 veintisiete	800 ochocient**os/as**
28 veintiocho	900 novecient**os/as**
29 veintinueve	1000 mil
30 treinta	1002 mil dos
31 treinta y uno	2000 dos mil
40 cuarenta	2300 dos mil trescientos
50 cincuenta	10.000 diez mil
60 sesenta	1.000.000 un millón

Examples

1984	mil novecientos ochenta y cuatro
2012	dos mil doce
2013	dos mil trece

Note:

- Doscientos/doscientas, trescientos/trescientas, cuatrocientos/cuatrocientas etc highlighted in the table above agrees with the noun in question.

doscientos chicos	two hundred boys
doscientas chicas	two hundred girls
doscientos euros	two hundred euros
doscientas rupias	two hundred rupees

GRAMMAR

Stress and Accents Marks

A key aspect of Spanish pronunciation is to know which syllable is to be stressed. There are three basic rules that govern the stress.

(A) If a word ends in a vowel (a, e, i, o, u), "n" or "s", the last but one syllable is stressed:

co**le**gio	school
se**ño**ra	lady
co**mi**da	food
e**xa**men	exam

Note: If a word ends in a vowel, "n" or "s" is NOT stressed on the last but one syllable, they have an accent on the stressed syllable:

e**xá**menes	exams
jóvenes	young people
último	last

(B) If a word ends in any other letter, the last syllable is stressed:

se**ñor**	Mr/ gentleman
ho**tel**	hotel
ciu**dad**	city

(C) If the word is not pronounced as per any of the above two rules it has to carry a written accent mark on the stressed syllable: A**mé**rica, ing**lés**, jar**dín**

However, the knowledge of which particular syllable is stressed in a word can only be acquired by practice and familiarity with the language.

TASKS AND EXERCISES

I. Read aloud the following registration numbers of Spanish cars. Take help from the above table with cardinal numbers:

B- 1262-MJ	M-8092-PF	Z-6259-TL	SE-6359-T
BI-4179-SO	SS-4159-MK	B-6309-LT	M-2747-OC

* **Model:** *be - uno, dos, seis, dos - eme, jota*

II. Imagine you are at a Train Reservation Counter and have to read aloud the spelling of your name:

*Model: ***Rosario Cerezal***:	*ere, o, ese, a, ere, i, o*	*Ce, e, ere, e, zeta, a, ele*

THE SPANISH SPEAKING WORLD

Spanish is the primary language spoken in many countries. One of these Spanish speaking countries is in Africa. Yes, Africa. Another one of the listed Spanish-speaking countries is in Europe. This European country colonized all the countries that presently speak Spanish. Sure you can guess which one it is!

All of the other Spanish-speaking countries are in Latin America. Latin America is made up of North, Central, and South American countries. The Caribbean is home to two Spanish-speaking countries. Here is a list of all these Spanish speaking countries:

Africa

EQUATORIAL GUINEA

Caribbean

CUBA

DOMINICAN REPUBLIC

Central America

COSTA RICA

EL SALVADOR

GUATEMALA

HONDURAS

NICARAGUA

PANAMA

Europe

SPAIN

North America

MEXICO

South America

ARGENTINA

BOLIVIA

CHILE

COLOMBIA

ECUADOR

PARAGUAY

PERU

URUGUAY

VENEZUELA

CHAPTER

2 Greetings

There are many ways to say hello in Spanish. Some expressions are best used in formal situations and others are more familiar in tone.

- ***Hola*** — Hello, hi — This greeting is suitable in both formal and informal contexts.
- ***Buenos días*** — Good day, good morning — In some areas, a shortened form, *buen día,* is used.
- ***Buenas tardes*** — Good afternoon, good evening — In most areas, *buenas tardes* should be used in the early evening in preference to *buenas noches.*
- ***Buenas noches*** — Good night — Unlike the English translation, *buenas noches* can be used as a greeting (late evening) as well as a farewell.

After an initial greeting, to ask about somebody's well being, you can ask the following questions:

- ***¿Cómo estás?/ ¿Cómo está?*** — How are you? — The first form (which is informal) normally would be used with someone you know on a first-name basis or when speaking with a child. The second form generally would be used in other situations.
- ***¿Cómo te va? ¿Cómo le va?*** — How's it going?— There is also a variety of colloquial alternatives uses, although many of them depend on the area. ***¿Qué tal? ¿Qué hay?---*** What's up? ***¿Qué pasa?*** — What's happening? ***¿Qué cuentas?*** - What's new?

Some typical responses to the above questions would be:

Estoy bien, gracias.¿Y tú?/ ¿Y usted? - I am fine, thank you. And how about you?

Muy bien – Very fine

Regular - So-so

There are several ways of saying "good bye" in Spanish, but the most common are the following two:

- ***Adiós*** – Goodbye – Is used for more lasting farewells
- ***Hasta luego*** - See you later – Is a more colloquial send off

While the above two expressions cover almost every situation, here are some more commonly used colloquial expressions:

- ***Nos vemos*** - See you around
- ***Chao*** – Bye
- ***Hasta mañana*** – See you tomorrow
- ***Hasta pronto*** – See you soon
- ***Buen fin de semana*** – Have a nice weekend
- ***Hasta el lunes/martes*** – See you on Monday/Tuesday

You must have noticed that while taking leave, you can use ***hasta***, meaning "until," with a time-expression to indicate when you will see that person next. You can use ***hasta*** with a week day (hasta + el lunes, hasta +el martes) to indicate which day of the week you are meeting the person.

Slightly more formal leave taking uses phrases such as the following:

- ***Que le vaya bien-*** Have a nice day -Used when the person you say it to is doing the leaving. If you are using the informal tone, it is ***Que te vaya bien***.

Dialogue:	**Diálogo:**
Greeting someone (informal)	
At the University	***En la universidad***
Gloria: Hello, Sania. How are you?	**Gloria:** ¡Hola, Sania! ¿Qué tal?
Sania: Very well. And how about you?	**Sania:** Muy bien. ¿Y tú?
Gloria: I am fine.	**Gloria:** Bien.
At a restaurant	***En un restaurante***
Juan: Hello, Kartik.	**Juan:** ¡Hola!, Kartik.
Kartik: Hello. How are you?	**Kartik:** ¡Hola! ¿Qué tal?
Greeting someone (formal)	
Just before the start of a meeting	***Al comienzo de una reunión***
Mrs. Gómez: Good morning. How are you, Mr. Torres?	**Señora Gómez:** Buenos días. ¿Cómo está, señor Torres?
Mr. Torres: Very well, thank you. And how about you?	**Señor Torres:** Muy bien, gracias. ¿Y usted?
Mrs. Gómez: Fine, thank you.	**Señora Gómez:** Bien, gracias.
At work	***En el trabajo***
Mr. Díaz: Good morning, Ms. Montes.	**Señor Díaz:** Buenos días, señorita Montes.
Ms. Montes: Good morning, Mr. Díaz. How are you?	**Señorita Montes:** Buenos días, señor Díaz. ¿Cómo le va?
Mr. Díaz: Very well, thank you.	**Señor Díaz:** Muy bien, gracias.
Taking leave of someone (formal)	
At the end of the day	***Al terminar el día***
Mr. Pérez: Good night, Mrs. Sáez.	**Señor Pérez:** Buenas noches, señora Sáez.
Mrs. Sáez: Bye. See you tomorrow.	**Señora Sáez:** Adiós. Hasta mañana.

Taking leave of someone (informal)	
In a restaurant	***En un restaurante***
Carmen: Bye, see you on Monday.	**Carmen:** Adiós, hasta el lunes.
Juan: Bye, Carmen. Have a nice weekend!	**Juan:** Adiós, Carmen. ¡Buen fin de semana!

VOCABULARY

Greetings

Hola	Hello/Hi
Buenos días; Buen día	Good day, Good morning
Buenas tardes	Good afternoon (used till early evening)
Buenas noches	Good night/Good evening (used as greeting at late evening)
¿Qué tal?	How are you?
¿Qué hay?; ¿Qué pasa?	What's up?

Taking Leave

Adiós	Good bye
Hasta la vista	See you
Hasta mañana	See you tomorrow
Hasta pronto/luego/el lunes	See you soon/later/on Monday

Days of the week

lunes	Monday
martes	Tuesday
miércoles	Wednesday
jueves	Thursday
viernes	Friday
sábado	Saturday
domingo	Sunday

GRAMMAR

Punctuation marks

There is not much difference in Spanish and English in their punctuation. But you must have noted a few upside-down question marks or exclamation points. In fact, the use of inverted question marks and exclamation points is a feature almost unique to Spanish. (They are also used in Galician, another official language of Spain).The inverted punctuation is used at the beginning of questions and exclamations. If only part of the sentence contains the question or exclamation, then they are used within the sentence. For example:

-¡Hola! ¿Qué tal?

- Buenos días, señor Torres. ¿Cómo está usted?

TASKS AND EXERCISES

I. Complete the following dialogue by supplying the missing words:

A. *Carmen*: - Buenos ...., señor Pérez. ¿Cómo .... usted?

Señor Pérez: Muy ...., gracias.

B. *Juan*: ¡Hola, Gloria! ¿Qué ....?

Gloria: ...... bien. ¿Y ......?

Juan: Bien.

C. *Señor Pérez*: Buenas........., señora Sáez.

Señora Sáez: - Adiós. .... mañana.

D. *Carmen*: ...., hasta el lunes.

Juan: Adiós, Carmen. ¡Buen.....................semana!

II. Write in Spanish what you would say in each of the following situations:

A. You enter office in the morning and greet your colleague.

____

B. It is Friday and one of your colleagues is leaving for home. Tell her/him that you will see her/him on Monday.

____

C. At the end of the dinner you want to say goodbye to your friends

____

D. Tell one of your friends to have a nice day

____

III. Read the following sentences and tell whether they are in formal tone or informal tone:

A. ¿Cómo estás? ....

B. ¿Cómo le va? ....

C. ¿Cómo está, señor Torres? ....

D. Bien, ¿Y tú? ....

E. ¡Que te vaya bien! ....

THE SPANISH SPEAKING WORLD

Tú/Usted

Spanish has both the informal and a formal way of addressing people. Therefore, Spanish speakers use two different forms of the pronoun "you": **tú** and **usted**. **Tú** is used in less formal modes of address while **usted** is formal.

Tú is used when you're talking to someone you are familiar with, someone of the same age or the same rank who you are acquainted with. You can also use it when you want to express a certain level of intimacy with someone though the person may be older. Most children in Spain use **tú** with their parents.

Usted is used for more formal occasions such as with a new acquaintance, an older person, or someone you consider to be of higher rank. It signifies a more respectful way of talking to someone.

At a fairly early point in a relationship between people who speak Spanish, a shift occurs from the formal **usted** to the more informal **tú** when they begin to use **tú** when addressing each other. In Spanish, we call this **tutearse** , that is, "to talk in **tú**." Of course, if you don't want to have a closer, more informal relationship with someone, or if you want to keep the tone professional, you should stick to using **usted** with that person.

Following are some examples of sentences that use **tú** and **usted**:

- **¿Cómo está usted?** : [How are you?] (Formal)
- **Gloria, ¿cómo estás?** [Gloria, how are you?] (Friendly, intimate)
- **Adiós, señor Torres, ¡Que le vaya bien!** [Good-bye Mr. Torres, have a nice day!] (Respectful, formal)

In written texts, the words **usted** and **ustedes** are often used in their abbreviated forms (**Ud.** and **Uds.**). When you read these abbreviations aloud, you say the whole word.

The informal and formal tones apply to the plural too but there are variations between Spain and Spanish America. When people in Spain want to address a group of people, they use the word **vosotros**, which is the informal "you" in the plural. Spanish-speaking Americans almost never use **vosotros**. They instead use **ustedes** (meaning "you," in the plural) which can be a formal way of addressing two or more people, or it can be very informal. The situation dictates the difference. Here are some examples:

- **¿Ustedes dos trabajan en Oracle?** [You both work in Oracle?] (Can be very informal or formal)
- **¿Usted es de Nueva Delhi?** [Are you from New Delhi?] (Formal)

REMEMBER

In Hispanic countries, it is customary for a woman to greet people by kissing them on the right cheek including in a business environment. Men normally greet each other by shaking hands.

CHAPTER

3

Getting to know people

¡Hola! ¿Cómo te llamas? Hello! What's your name?

¡Hola! Me llamo	Hello! My name is ....

Enrique	Manolo	Carmen	María	Alberto
Sergio	Rafael	Julio	Cristina	Ana
Felipe	Juan	Consuelo	Carlos	Fernando
Pablo	Luis	Víctor	José Manuel	Rosalía

Put an "F" in front of names that you think are that of women and an "M" in front of those you think are men's.

These are some of the commonest first names (**nombre**) in Spanish. In the Spanish-speaking world, it is customary to have two surnames (**apellidos**), the first is the father's surname and the second is the mother's surname (used mainly in written documents). Let us look at the following examples:

List of Spanish University Students coming to India on a Study India Tour

Nombre	Apellidos
Fernando	Cerezal Sierra
Rosario	Diez Cabrera
Antonio	García Torres
Pablo	Gómez Martín
Adela	González Olmos
José María	Gutiérrez Alonso
Mercedes	López Velarde
Ana María	Muñoz Salazar
Cristina	Núñez Saldaña

Dialogue:	**Diálogo:**
Meeting someone for the first time (informal)	
At the University	***En la universidad***
Cristina: Hello! My name is Cristina.	**Cristina:** ¡Hola! Me llamo Cristina.
Sania: Hello! I am Sania. Are you from Latin America?	**Sania:** ¡Hola! Yo soy Sania. ¿Eres de América Latina?
Cristina: Yes, I am from Venezuela, from Caracas. I am a student.	**Cristina:** Sí, soy de Venezuela, de Caracas. Soy estudiante.
Sania: I am a student too. I study Spanish and you. What's your name?	**Sania:** Yo también soy estudiante. Estudio español. Y tú, ¿cómo te llamas?
Felipe: Hi, I am Felipe.	**Felipe:** ¡Hola! Yo soy Felipe.
Meeting someone for the first time (formal)	
At the Airport	***En el aeropuerto***
Kapil: Good Morning. Are you Mr. Torres?	**Kapil:** Buenos Días. ¿Es Ud. el señor Torres?
Torres: Yes. That's me.	**Torres:** Sí. Soy yo.
Kapil: My name is Kapil and I am the secretary of Mrs. Rosario Cerezal.	**Kapil:** Me llamo Kapil y soy el secretario de la señora Rosario Cerezal.
Torres: Pleased to meet you.	**Torres:** Encantado.
Kapil: The pleasure is mine.	**Kabir:** Mucho gusto.
Introducing someone (informal)	
In a restaurant	**En un restaurante**
Carmen: Juan, look, this is my friend Kartik. He is from New Delhi. He is a programmer. He works in "Oracle."	**Carmen:** Juan, mira, éste es mi amigo Kartik. Es de Nueva Delhi. Es programador. Trabaja en "Oracle."
Juan: Hello, Kartik	**Juan:** ¡Hola!, Kartik.
Kartik: Hello. How do you do	Kartik: ¡Hola! ¿Qué tal?

Introducing someone (formal)	
At a reception in the Chamber of Commerce in Madrid	**En la recepción de la Cámara de Comercio en Madrid**
Mr. González: Mr. Olmos, this is Mrs. Martín, the Commercial director of "Canon."	**Sr. González:** Señor Olmos, ésta es la señora Martín, la directora comercial de "Canon."
Sr. Olmos: Pleased to meet you.	**Sr. Olmos:** Mucho gusto.
Sra. Martín: Pleased to meet you too.	**Sra. Martín:** Encantada.

VOCABULARY

Introducing/Meeting someone	
Éste es (masc) / Ésta es (fem)	This is ...
¡Hola! Mucho gusto.	Hello! It's a pleasure to meet you
Encantado/	Delighted to meet you
(Encantad**a** if the speaker is a female)	
Giving/Seeking Personal Information	
Name	
¿Cómo te llamas?	What's your name?
Me llamo María/Cristina/Juan...	My name is María/Cristina/Juan...
Soy María/Cristina/Juan...	I am María/Cristina/Juan...
¿Es usted el Sr./la Sra. ...?	Are you Mr./Mrs. ...
Profession	
Soy...	I am
Trabajo en	I work in...
Juan trabaja en	Juan works in...
Estudio...	I study
Profesor (masculine)/ Profesora (feminine)	Professor
Médico/ Médica	Doctor
Ingeniero/ Ingeniera	Engineer
Estudiante	Student

Nationality/Origin	
Soy de ...	I am from....
¿Eres de...?	Are you from...?
Es de	He/She is from ...
Soy indio(masculine)/ india (feminine)	I am Indian
Soy español(masculine)/ española	I am Spanish

Note: In order to know more about countries and nationality, refer to the additional vocabulary.

GRAMMAR

I. Subject Pronouns (They replace the subject of a sentence)

I	**yo**
you	**tú**(familiar)
you	**usted (Ud.)** (formal)
he, she	**él, ella**
we	**nosotros** (m), **nosotras** (f) (the first form refers to a group of males or males and females, while the second form refers to females only)
you all	**vosotros** (m), **vosotras** (f) (familiar; the first form refers to a group of males or males and females, while the second form refers to females only; this pronoun is seldom used in most parts of Latin America)
you all	**ustedes (Uds.)** (formal in Spain, informal in Spanish America)
they	**ellos** (m), **ellas** (f)

To Use or not to Use Subject Pronouns

Unlike in English where it is necessary to use them, in Spanish subject pronouns are often left out. In some specific contexts their use is essential, but when they're not necessary using them would amount to overuse. Why does this happen? Because in Spanish the verb forms often make it clear who the subject is, and when that's the case the pronouns shouldn't be used unless there's a reason to.

Here are examples of sentences where pronouns are unnecessary:

***Trabajo** en un hospital* [**I work** in a hospital]: Here the verb form *Trabajo* (first person of *trabajar*, ie, to work) can refer only to the person speaking.

*¿**Eres** de España?*[**Are you** from Spain?]: Here the verb *Eres* (second person of ser, ie to be) can only refer to the person being spoken to.

Unlike other subject pronouns, the pronouns **usted** and **ustedes** are generally used with the corresponding verb forms.

II. Demonstrative Pronouns (Replace a noun while also pointing at it. Used in introductions)

This is Mario.	**Éste es** Mario.
This is Maria.	**Ésta es** María.
These are Mario and Claudia.	**Éstos son** Mario y Claudia.
These are Claudia and Maria.	**Éstas son** Claudia y María.

III. Verbs

As you have seen above, verbs in Spanish not only contain information about the action, but also who performed the action (the *subject*). The conjugations of verbs are, therefore, very important in Spanish and in order to speak and write Spanish properly, you are going to have to learn how to **conjugate** the verbs.

Are you ready to learn more?

A. The verb SER (to be) is used to tell name, profession, nationality and is therefore a very useful verb when you are giving information about yourself or seeking information about somebody. The "Presente de Indicativo" (present tense) of "ser" is conjugated as follows:

(yo)	soy
(tú)	eres
(usted/él/ella)	es
(nosotros/as)	somos
(vosotros/as)	sois
(ustedes/ellos/ellas)	son

You must have noted that the formal **usted** (you) is conjugated like the third person singular **él/ella** (he/she) and **ustedes** is conjugated like third person plural **ellos/ellas**.

B. All Spanish verbs can be divided into three groups depending on their ending:

1st group: verbs ending in 'ar'

2nd group: verbs ending in 'er '

3rd group: verbs ending in 'ir'

While some verbs like "ser" above are **irregular**, others are **regular** and follow a fixed pattern of conjugation. Let us look at the table below to see the conjugations of regular –ar, -er and –ir ending verbs in the Presente de indicativo:

	trabajar (to work)	comer (to eat)	vivir (to live)
Yo	trabaj**o**	com**o**	viv**o**
Tú	trabaj**as**	com**es**	viv**es**
Ud./él/ella	trabaj**a**	com**e**	viv**e**
Nosotros/as	trabaj**amos**	com**emos**	viv**imos**
Vosotros/as	trabaj**áis**	com**éis**	viv**ís**
Uds./ellos/ellas	trabaj**an**	com**en**	viv**en**

As you can see from the above table, the infinitive form (non-conjugated form) of the verb like **trabajar**, **comer**, **vivir**, consists of a root (**trabaj**-, **com**-, **viv**-) and a stem (the ending: **-ar**, **-er** or **-ir**). To conjugate a regular verb, we remove the stem, ie, the endings, and add the suffixes in the pattern highlighted above to the root.

C. Here are some regular verbs of common use:

- ar		**- er**		**-ir**	
hablar	*to speak*	leer	*to read*	escribir	*to write*
viajar	*to travel*	beber	*to drink*	abrir	*to open*
descansar	*to rest*	vender	*to sell*	recibir	*to receive*
comprar	*to buy*	aprender	*to learn*	subir	*to climb*
visitar	*to visit*	comprender	*to understand*	cubrir	*to cover*
pagar	*to pay*	correr	*to run*	partir	*to leave*

D. Uses of the Present Tense

Following are the different ways the simple present tense (presente de indicativo) is used in Spanish.

- **To describe an action that is repeated habitually or regularly or to tell a general truth :**

Pedro habla español y portugués.	Pedro speaks Spanish and Portuguese
Descanso mucho los sábados.	I rest a lot on Saturdays
María escribe bien.	María writes well
Ella es inteligente.	She is intelligent

- **To describe something that is happening now.**

Ella aprende español.	She is learning Spanish
Él trabaja en Infosys.	He is working in Infosys

- **To describe something happening in the near future:** In both English and Spanish, the present and future tenses are often interchangeable for this purpose. Generally a time marker is indicated in the sentence for this usage of the present as future.

El tren parte a las ocho de la noche.	The train leaves at 8 p.m.
Él visita Delhi la semana próxima.	He is visiting Delhi next week
El banco abre mañana.	The bank will open tomorrow

- **In questions, to get instructions:** In English, such a usage often uses the verb "do."

¿Pago ahora o después?	Do I pay now or later?
¿Dónde escribo mi nombre?	Where do I write my name?

TASKS AND EXERCISES

I. Mrs. Rosario Cerezal is the Manager of the New Delhi office of a Mexico based Telecommunications firm (Mundivisión SA). Look at her identity card in Spanish. Make an Identity card in Spanish for yourself filling in the relevant details using the same model.

Nombre : Rosario **Apellidos**: Cerezal Sierra **Nacionalidad**: mexicana **Empresa** : **Mundivisión SA** **Fecha de nacimiento**: 03/08/1957	**Nombre** : ____________ **Apellidos**: ____________ **Nacionalidad**: indio/ india **Empresa** : ____________ **Fecha de nacimiento**: _____

II. In the dialogue given below, you have to choose the correct answer.

Hola

- ¿Cómo te llamas?

- ¿Kumar es tu apellido o tu nombre?

  ____

- ¿Eres indio?

  ____

- ¿Dónde trabajas?

  ____

- ¿Y tu número de teléfono?

  ____

Apellido.
Es el 8824576801.
Me llamo Arun Kumar.
Sí, soy indio.
En la empresa IBM.

Muchas Gracias. Hasta luego.

III. Complete the following table:

	Hablar	Trabajar	Escribir	Llamarse	Ser
(Yo)	hablo			me llamo	soy
(Tú)				te	
(Ud, él, ella)				se	es
(Nosotros)				nos	
(Vosotros)		trabajáis		os	
(Uds,ellos/as)			escriben	se	

THE SPANISH SPEAKING WORLD

Forms of address

The titles señor (Mr.), señora (Mrs.) and señorita (Miss) are used in front of the person's surname in the formal mode of address. They are usually abbreviated and written as: **Sr., Sra.** and **Srta.** You have to use the definite article **el,** or **la** in front of the titles except when you are directly addressing the person.

Mr. Olmos is the Manager.	El Sr. Olmos es el gerente.
Mr. Olmos, Good Morning.	Sr. Olmos, Buenos días.
Mrs. Cerezal is from Argentina.	La Sra. Cerezal es de Argentina.
Thank you, Mrs. Cerezal.	Gracias, Sra. Cerezal.

Sometimes the titles **Don** and **Doña** are also used in the formal mode of address but they are followed not by the surname, but the first name: **Don Juan, Doña Inés**.

CHAPTER

Meeting professionals

Below you will find the Spanish names of some of the professions. Do they sound familiar to you?

Gerente **Médico**

INGENIERO

Profesora **Mecánico**

Piloto **Agricultor**

Taxista

In Spanish, many professions end in –or/ ora, ero/era or –ista like:

Doctor-a (doctor)	Peluquero-a (hairstylist)	Periodista (journalist)
Agricultor-a (farmer)	Jardinero-a (gardener)	Taxista (taxi driver)
Conductor-a (driver)	Cocinero-a (cook)	Dentista (dentist)

But there are many which end in just -o/-a (-o is masculine, -a is feminine):

Psicólogo-a (psychologist)	Mecánico-a (mechanic)
Cirujano-a (surgeon)	

The professions which just end in -e and -ista do not change and remain same for feminine and masculine:

Cantante (singer)	Estudiante (student)
Ayudante (assistant)	

Dialogue:	**Diálogo:**
In an office	***En una oficina***
Shiv: Hello! Ramon. Let me introduce you to Sanjay. He is an economist.	**Shiv:** ¡Hola! Ramón.Te presento a Sanjay. Es economista.
Ramon: Nice to meet you, Sanjay.	**Ramón:** Mucho gusto, Sanjay.
In an interview	***En una entrevista***
Shanti: What do you do?	**Shanti:** ¿A qué te dedicas?
Rodrigo: I am a waiter.	**Rodrigo:** Soy camarero.
Shanti: Where do you work?	**Shanti:** ¿Dónde trabajas?
Rodrigo: I work in the Arcoiris restaurant.	**Rodrigo:** Trabajo en el restaurante Arcoíris.
Shanti: Where is this restaurant?	**Shanti:** ¿Dónde está este restaurante?
Rodrigo: It is on the Simón Bolivar street.	**Rodrigo:** Está en la calle Simón Bolivar.
Two professionals speak	***Hablan dos profesionales***
Saloni: Carmen, what do you work as?	**Saloni:** Carmen, ¿en qué trabajas?
Carmen: I work as a nurse in the hospital. And you?	**Carmen:** Trabajo de enfermera en el hospital. ¿Y tú?
Saloni: I work as a cook in Indian Spice restaurant.	**Saloni:** Yo trabajo de cocinera en el restaurante Indian Spice.
Carmen: Are there many Indian restaurants here in Buenos Aires?	**Carmen:** ¿Hay muchos restaurantes indios aquí en Buenos Aires?
Saloni: Yes, there are more than ten.	**Saloni:** Sí, hay más de diez.
Meeting a friend	***Encuentro con un amigo***
Shiv: Good Morning, Rodrigo. How are things?	**Shiv:** Buenos días, Rodrigo. ¿Qué hay?

Rodriguez: Very well, Shiv. These days I am working as a teacher in a school.	**Rodrigo:** Muy bien, Shiv. Estos días trabajo como profesor en un colegio.
Shiv: That's great! But aren't you an engineer?	**Shiv:** ¡Qué bien! Pero tú eres ingeniero, ¿no?
Rodrigo: Yes, but I no longer work as an engineer. I love teaching children.	**Rodrigo:** Sí, pero ya no trabajo de ingeniero. Me encanta enseñar a los niños.

VOCABULARY

Soy...	I am...
Trabajar en....	To work at.......
Trabajar de/ trabajar como	To work as......
¿A qué te dedicas?	What do you do?
¿En qué trabajas?	What do you do?
Gerente	Manager
Abogado/Abogada	Lawyer
Político/ Política	Politician
Científico/ Científica	Scientist
Escritor/ Escritora	Writer

While seeking informations, we use interrogatives. Below are some of the commonly used interrogatives in Spanish.

Qué (what, which)	
¿Qué haces?	What are you doing?
¿Qué restaurante prefieres?	Which restaurant do you prefer?
Cuándo (when)	
¿Cuándo termina la reunión?	When does the meeting end?
Dónde (where)	
¿Dónde trabajas?	Where do you work?
¿ Dónde está ...?	Where is ....?
Por qué (why)	
¿Por qué estudias español?	Why do you study Spanish?

Quién (who)	
¿Quién es él?	Who is he?
Cómo (how)	
¿Cómo estás?	How are you?
Cuánto/Cuánta (how much/ how many)	
¿Cuánto tiempo necesitas?	How much time do you need?
¿Cuánta gente trabaja aquí?	How many people work here?
Cuántos/Cuántas (how many)	
¿Cuántos empleados hay en este hospital?	How many employees are there in this hospital?
¿Cuántas empresas indias hay en Buenos Aires?	How many Indian companies are there in Buenos Aires?

GRAMMAR

I. Noun

1. In Spanish, every noun is either masculine or feminine. The noun that ends with ***o*** is generally masculine.

   el periódic**o** (the magazine)

   el aeropuert**o** (the airport)

   el chic**o** (the boy)

Exceptions: There are a few exceptions to this rule. Some nouns that end with ***o*** are feminine. For example, **la foto** (the photo), **la mano** (the hand), **la moto** (the motorcycle).

2. The noun that ends with **a**, **sión, ción**, **dad** are generally feminine.

   la chic**a** (the girl)

   la cart**a** (the letter)

   la televi**sión** (the television)

   la lec**ción** (the lesson)

   la ciu**dad** (the city)

Exceptions: There are a few exceptions to this rule. Some nouns that end with **a** are masculine. For example, **el clima** (the climate), **el día** (the day), **el sistema** (the system), **el problema** (the problem).

3. Those which refer to a living being can easily be classified in male or female. In Spanish, the nouns which end in **o** can be changed to feminine by changing the ending to **a**.

el chico	the boy	la chica	the girl
el tío	the uncle	la tía	the aunt

Note: Some nouns have different words for male and female. For example:

el padre	the father	la madre	the mother
el hombre	the man	la mujer	the woman

As far as the non living objects are concerned, one has to learn their grammatical gender. The examples given below will help you to understand it better.

el pasaporte	the passport	la ciudad	the city
el cuaderno	the notebook	el hotel	the hotel

Forming the plural of the nouns is easy. Just remember that the nouns which end in a vowel add **s** to them, nouns which end in a consonant add **es** to them. For example:

Singular	Plural	Singular	Plural
el pasaporte	los pasaportes	la ciudad	las ciudades
el cuaderno	los cuadernos	el hotel	los hoteles

II. Articles

In English the articles are *a, an,* and *the* which generally go with a noun. Articles are of two types: Definite Article and Indefinite article.

1. Definite Article

In English there is only one definite article – *the.* But in Spanish the same article *the* has four forms depending on the number and gender of the object: **el, la, los, las**.

El is used with masculine singular nouns: el chico (the boy)

La is used with feminine singular nouns: la chica (the girl)

Los is used with masculine plural nouns: los chicos. (the boys)

Las is used with feminine plural nouns: las chicas (the girls)

Note:

- If the preposition **a** which means **to** is followed by the definite article **el**, then the two words combine and become **al (a + el)**.

al mercado — to the market

al teatro — to the theatre

➢ If the preposition **de** which means **of/from** is followed by the definite article **el** then the two words combine and become **del (de + el)**.

del libro — of/from the book

del escritor — of/from the writer

2. Indefinite Article

The Indefinite article in English are – *a, an* and in plural we use *some.* In Spanish the indefinite article has four forms: **un, una, unos, unas**.

Un is used with masculine singular nouns: un chico (a boy)

Una is used with feminine singular nouns: una chica (a girl)

Unos is used with masculine plural nouns: unos chicos. (some boys)

Unos is used with feminine plural nouns: unas chicas (some girls)

III. Irregular Verbs: Ser, Estar, Hay

You have already learnt the verb *Ser* in the previous chapter. There is another irregular verb called *Estar*. The two verbs *Ser* and *Estar* have got the same meaning *to be*. A lot has been written about these two verbs. The conjugation of both these verbs is given in the table:

Subject Pronoun	**Ser** (to be)	**Estar** (to be)	
(yo)	soy	estoy	I am
(tú)	eres	estás	you are
(él/ell/usted)	es	está	he/she/it is, you are
(nosotros/as)	somos	estamos	we are
(vosotros/as)	sois	estáis	you are
(ellos/ellas/ustedes)	son	están	they/you are

1. **Ser is used:**

➢ To talk about nationality, to describe any person, place, to talk about the permanent qualities of anything.

Soy indio/a. — I am an Indian.

Ella es alta y guapa. — She is tall and pretty.

Delhi es una ciudad famosa. — Delhi is a famous city.

La mesa es redonda.	The table is round.

➢ To talk about the profession.

Somos estudiantes.	We are students.
Él es camarero.	He is a waiter.
Soy médico.	I am a doctor.

➢ For telling time

¿Qué hora es?	What time is it?
Son las dos.	Its two o'clock.

➢ To denote possession.

El libro es de Juan.	It's John's books.
Es mi casa.	It's my house.

➢ With adjectives such as necessary (necesario), important (importante), dificult (difícil) when the subject of the sentence is *it*.

Es necesario.	It is necessary.
Es importante.	It is important.
Es difícil.	It is difficult.

2. Estar is used:

➢ To talk about location of something or someone.

Estoy en Barcelona.	I am in Bercelona.
Barcelona está en España.	Barcelona is in Spain.

➢ To ask people how they are.

¿Cómo estás?	How are you?
Estoy bien.	I am fine.

➢ To express temporary state or condition.

El té está frio.	The tea is cold.
Raul está muy guapo hoy.	Raul is looking handsome today.

➢ With some fixed expressions.

Estar de vacaciones (to be on holiday)

Estoy de vacaciones.	I am on holiday.

Estar de acuerdo (to agree)

Estoy de acuerdo con él.	I agree with him.

- With *gerunds* which denotes the present continuous tense.

  Estoy comiendo ahora. I am eating now.

3. **Hay:** *Hay* means there is / there are. While *Estar* denotes the location, the verb hay denotes the existance of something.

For example:

¿Hay un banco por aquí cerca?	Is there any bank near here?
Hay muchos empleados en la empresa.	There are many employees in the company.
El Banco Central está en la calle Benito Juarez.	The Central Bank is on Benito Juarez Street.

TASKS AND EXERCISES

I. Complete the dialogues.

1. ¡Hola! ¿A qué te dedicas?

   .... médico. ¿Y ustedes?

   Nosotros..........................cirujanos.

2. ¡Oye! ¿Dónde............el Banco Central?

   Está en la Plaza de España.

3. ¿Cuántos hoteles hay en el centro?

   .... quince hoteles.

II. Fill in the blanks with the verb *Ser, Estar* or *Hay*.

1. Dinesh......................estudiante.
2. Ellos...........................de vacaciones en Italia.
3. ....cinco abogados en la habitación.
4. La comida.................fría.
5. Vosotras...........................alemanas.
6. ....muchas tiendas en Connaught Place.

III. Find the name of eight jobs and professions in the puzzle.

Y	N	J	Q	D	S	Y	D	Y	P	E	M	J	P	N
G	K	C	C	P	K	L	J	O	B	S	I	W	I	U
A	G	R	I	C	U	L	T	O	R	T	J	B	L	Z
V	O	S	O	U	O	C	I	W	O	U	V	J	O	G
C	C	X	W	E	Z	E	V	B	A	D	N	V	T	X
W	W	R	Q	V	T	O	K	G	Q	I	Q	T	O	X
X	J	V	J	N	U	N	R	L	T	A	Q	G	E	P
C	G	G	E	R	E	N	T	E	A	N	T	S	T	U
A	F	R	E	R	C	Z	V	I	M	T	E	T	N	J
N	E	N	U	U	A	T	S	I	D	E	I	R	E	P
T	B	W	L	Z	L	I	D	O	N	A	N	T	E	V
A	Y	T	A	X	I	S	T	A	R	J	T	E	E	Z
N	O	U	E	O	I	W	S	B	T	B	A	S	W	M
T	Y	Q	L	U	Z	N	Y	D	S	L	A	I	E	C
E	Y	P	K	A	P	E	R	I	O	D	I	S	T	A

THE SPANISH SPEAKING WORLD

Latin America and Spain have produced several creative people in various fields, be it arts or literature. You might already know these famous personalities whose short biographies are given below.

Miguel de Cervantes Saavedra

He was a 16th century Spanish writer. His work *Don Quijote de la Mancha* is considered to be the first modern novel in the European literary history. It was published in two parts, first in 1605 and second in 1615. It is a parody of the chivalric novels but also a criticism of the Spanish society of that time. It is one of the most translated books of all times.

Gabriel García Márquez

Gabriel García Márquez is a Colombian novelist and journalist. He is considered to be one of the most important authors of Latin America. He was awarded the Nobel Prize for literature in 1982. His book *Cien años de soledad* (One Hundred Years of Solitude), published in 1967, is considered to be a masterpiece.

Salma Hayek

Salma Hayek Jiménez, popularly known as Salma Hayek, is a Mexican film actress. She was born on September 2, 1966 in Coatzacoalcos, Mexico. Her depiction of the Mexican painter Frida Kahlo in the film *Frida* won her many accolades and awards.

Pedro Almodóvar

Pedro Almodóvar Caballero, born in a small town in the region of La Mancha of Spain, is an internationally acclaimed film director and producer. He is considered to be one of the most successful Spanish film makers. His first international success came from the movie called *Mujeres al borde de un ataque de nervios* (Women on the Verge of a Nervous Breakdown). His other famous movie is *Volver* for which the Spanish actress Penélope Cruz received an Oscar nomination for Best Actress in 2006.

CHAPTER

5 Family and friends

The next important thing to know for us is to talk about family and friends. Below is a brief description about the *García* family.

Un pequeño texto sobre la familia García:

Almudena y Ramón tienen dos hijos. Se llaman Pedro y Silvia. Pedro está casado con Dolores y ellos tienen una hija de seis meses. Pedro es taxista y Dolores trabaja en una farmacia. Silvia tiene un novio, Jorge, quien es futbolista. Silvia es diseñadora gráfica. Ramón y Almudena ya no trabajan. Ellos están jubilados. Ellos también tienen una perrita mascota Necha que tiene dos años. Los García son una familia pequeña y alegre.

A small text on the García family:

Almudena and Ramón have two children. Their names are Pedro and Sylvia. Pedro is married to Dolores and they have a daughter of six months. Pedro is a taxi driver and Dolores works in a pharmacy. Silvia has a boyfriend, Jorge who is a footballer. Silvia is a graphic designer. Ramón and Almudena no longer work. They are retired. They also have a pet dog Necha who is two years old. The Garcias are a small and happy family.

Su árbol geneológico **Their family tree**

Almudena Álvarez Arocas + Ramón García Gómez

+

Silvia García Álvarez Pedro García Álvarez Dolores Llanos Rodríguez

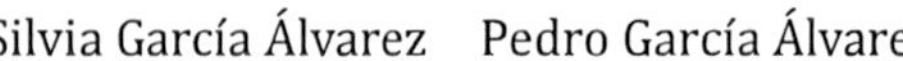

Sofía Álvarez Llanos

From the above family tree, you can determine the familial relationships as well as see how the Spanish surnames are taken.

Silvia es la **hija** de Almudena y Ramón.	Silvia is the **daughter** of Almudena and Ramón.
Pedro es el hijo de **los García***.	Pedro is the son of **the Garcias.**

**(In Spanish, if we refer to the entire family of someone, we take the name of the surname of the father and combine it with the third person plural masculine definite article los. Eg. Los García, los Rodriguez as in English the Smiths, the Simpsons, the Jones).*

Dolores is **his** wife.	Dolores es **su** esposa.
His daughter´s name is Sofía.	**Su** hija se llama Sofía.
Silvia and Pedro are brothers and sisters.	Silvia y Pedro son hermanos.
Dolores is the sister-in-law of Silvia.	Dolores es la cuñada de Silvia.

Almudena is Dolores′ mother-in-law.	Almudena es la suegra de Dolores.
Dolores is the daughter-in-law of Ramon and Almudena.	Dolores es la nuera de Ramón y Almudena.

Dialogue:	**Diálogo:**
In the cafeteria of the faculty:	***En la cafetería de la facultad:***
Pepe: Hi Rodrigo! What's up?	**Pepe:** ¡Hola Rodrigo! ¿Qué hay?
Rodrigo: Hey man! I am alright! How you doing?	**Rodrigo:** Hombre! ¡Muy bien! ¿Cómo andas?
Pepe: Hey, this is my sister Julia. She is studying architecture.	**Pepe:** Oye, te presento a mi hermana Julia. Estudia arquitectura.
Rodrigo: Nice to meet you Julia. Do you study here at our university?	**Rodrigo:** Mucho gusto, Julia. ¿Estudias aquí en nuestra universidad?
Julia: No, I study at Complutense as the Faculty of Architecture is very good there.	**Julia:** No, estudio en la Complutense ya que la Facultad de Arquitectura es muy buena allí.
Rodrigo: What a coincidence! My younger brother also goes to Complutense, but my elder sister works in a multinational company.	**Rodrigo:** ¡Qué casualidad! Mi hermano menor también va a la Complutense, pero mi hermana mayor trabaja en una empresa multinacional.
Pepe: Well, all right. Rodrigo, let's have a coffee and talk. I invite you.	**Pepe:** Pues, muy bien. Rodrigo, vamos a tomar un café y hablamos. Te invito yo.
Amanda and Irina are two friends who are meeting in a supermarket after a long time. Amanda tells Irina about her boyfriend.	***Amanda e Irina son dos amigas que se encuentran en el supermercado. Amanda le cuenta de su novio.***
Amanda: Hi Irina! How are you? So long!	**Amanda:** Hola Irina! ¿Qué tal? ¡Tanto tiempo!

Irina: I am very good, Amanda, and you? What´s up with you?	**Irina:** Muy bien, Amanda, ¿y tú? ¿Cómo te va?
Amanda: Fine. How pretty you look! It´s been long since we have not seen each other.	**Amanda:** Bien. ¡Qué guapa estás! Hace mucho que no nos vemos.
Irina: Thanks. Tell me, do you have a boyfriend?	**Irina:** Gracias. Cuéntame ¿ya tienes novio?
Amanda: Yes, his name is Ruben. He studies in the University.	**Amanda:** Sí, se llama Rubén. Estudia en la Universidad.
Irina: How is he?	**Irina:** ¿Cómo es?
Amanda: He is very nice and affectionate.	**Amanda:** Es muy majo y cariñoso.
Irina: Really?, and how does he look?	**Irina:** ¿Ah sí? y ¿qué aspecto tiene él?
Amanda: He is tall, lean, dark haired and has light coloured eyes. He also wears glasses.	**Amanda:** Es alto, delgado, moreno y tiene ojos claros. También lleva gafas.
Irina: Wow!	**Irina:** ¡Qué bien!

VOCABULARY

La familia	Family
El padre	Father
La madre	Mother
El hijo, la hija	Son, daughter
El hermano, la hermana	Brother, sister
El tío, la tía	Uncle, aunt
El primo, la prima	Cousin
El sobrino, la sobrina	Nephew, niece
El abuelo, la abuela	Grandfather, grandmother
El nieto, la nieta	Grandson, granddaughter
El marido, la mujer	Wife, husband
El suegro, la suegra	Father in law, mother in law
El yerno, la nuera	Son in law, daughter in law

Note: In order to say the plural of any relation, for eg., parents, children, grandparents etc, take the masculine singular of any relation and make its plural. For example:

Los padres: parents

Los hijos: children

Los abuelos: grandparents

El cuñado, la cuñada	Brother in law, sister in law
Los parientes	Relatives

Estado Civil - Marital Status

Estar casado/a: (to be married)	Estoy casado.	I am married.
Estar divorciado/a: (to be divorced)	Ella está divorciada.	She is divorced.
Estar separado/a: (to be separated)	Estamos separados.	We are separated.
Ser soltero /a : (to be single)	Soy soltero.	I am single.

Aspectos físicos	**Physical aspects**
Alto/alta	Tall
Gordo/gorda	Fat
Feo/fea	Ugly
Delgado/delgada	Slim
Guapo/guapa	Handsome/pretty
Bajo/baja	Short
Joven	Young
Viejo/vieja	Old
Atractivo/atractiva	Attractive
Calvo/calva	Bald
Rubio/rubia	Blonde
Moreno/morena	Dark haired/ dark skinned
Tener el pelo corto/ largo/rizado/ liso	To have short/long/curly/straight hair
Tengo el pelo corto	I have short hair
Llevar gafas	To wear glasses
No llevo gafas	I don't wear glasses.

GRAMMAR

I. Adjectives

An adjective is a word that describes a noun. For example, good, bad, tall, green, handsome.

A. In Spanish the adjective generally follows the noun. It has four forms. For example, see the forms of the adjective *alto* (tall).

	Singular	**Plural**
Masculine	alto	altos
Feminine	alta	altas

B. As we have just seen, in Spanish the adjectives agrees with the gender and number of the noun. That is, the adjective will change depending on whether the noun one is referring to is masculine, feminine, singular or plural.

un libro caro.	an expensive book.
una casa barata.	a cheap house.
unos chicos altos.	some tall boys.
unas chicas guapas.	some pretty girls.

1. Possessive adjectives

They denote possession or belonging.

The possessive adjectives in English are "my", "your", "his", "her", "our", "your", "their" which tells who owns or possesses something. In Spanish they are **mi/mis, tu/tus, su/sus, nuestro/a, nuestros/ nuestras, vuestro/a, vuestros/as, su/sus**.

Singular		**Plural**	
Masculine	*Feminine*	*Masculine*	*Feminine*
Mi amigo		**Mis** amigos	
My friend		My friends	
Tu padre		**Tus** padres	
Your father		Your parents	
Su abuelo		**Sus** abuelos	
Your/his/her grandfather		Your/his/her grandparents	
Nuestro tío	**Nuestra** tía	**Nuestros** tíos	**Nuestras** tías
Our uncle	Our aunt	Our uncles and aunts	Our aunts

Vuestro hermano	**Vuestra** hermana	**Vuestros** hermanos	**Vuestras** hermanas
Your brother	Your sister	Your brothers and sisters	Your sisters
Su familia		**Sus** familias	
Your/their family		Your/their families	
As you can see, the possessive adjectives are same for both masculine and feminine except in *nosotros/as* and *vosotros/as* form. In these two forms it agrees not only with number but also gender of the noun as shown above.			

2. Demonstrative adjectives

The demonstrative adjective is used to point out something or someone. In English they are *this, that, these* and *those*. In Spanish the demonstrative adjectives change according to number and gender of the noun. See the table below.

	Masculine	**Feminine**	
singular	este	esta	this
plural	estos	estas	these
singular	ese	esa	that(a little far)
plural	esos	esas	those(a little far)
singular	aquel	aquella	that (quite far)
plural	aquellos	aquellas	those(quite far)

- Este/esta/estos/estas are used when the object is near the speaker. For example:

Este libro es muy famoso.	This book is very famous.
Esta camisa es buena.	This shirt is good.
Estos libros son muy famosos.	These books are very famous.
Estas camisas son buenas.	These shirts are good.

- Ese/esa/esos/esas are used when the object is a little far from the speaker. For example:

Ese chico es inteligente.	That boy is intelligent.
Esa chica es guapa.	That girl is pretty.

Esos chicos son inteligentes.	Those boys are intelligent.
Esas chicas son guapas.	Those girls are pretty.

- Aquel/aquella/aquellos/aquellas are used when the object is quite far from the speaker. For example:

Aquel edificio es muy barato.	That building is very cheap.
Aquella casa es muy cara.	That house is very expensive.
Aquellos edificios son muy baratos.	Those buildings are very cheap.
Aquellas casas son muy caras.	Those houses are very expensive.

II. Irregular verbs

By now you are familiar with the regular verbs and some irregular verbs that we have seen in the previous chapters. Let's learn some more.

1. The verb **tener** (to have) is also used frequently in our day to day life.

	Tener (to have)
Yo	tengo
Tú	tienes
Ud./él/ella	tiene
Nosotros/as	tenemos
Vosotros/as	tenéis
Uds./ellos/ellas	tienen

Examples:

Tengo dos hijos. I have two children.

No tengo novia. I don't have a girlfriend.

Ella tiene el pelo largo. She has long hair.

➢ The verb **Tener** is also used with some fixed expressions. Some of them are given below:

- Tener hambre (to be hungry)

  Tengo hambre. I am hungry.

- Tener sed (to be thirsty)

  No tenemos sed. We are not thirsty.

- Tener calor (to feel hot)

  Ellos tienen calor. They are feeling hot.

- Tener frío.

  ¿Tienes frio? Are you feeling cold?

- Tener sueño (to be sleepy)

  Él tiene sueño. He is feeling sleepy.

- Tener prisa (to be in a hurry)

  Ella tiene prisa. She is in a hurry.

- Tener............años (to be ...old)

  ¿Cuántos años tienes? How old are you?

  Tengo 20 años. I am 20 years old.

2. **In the table given below there are few more irregular verbs with examples.**

	Hacer (to do/ to make)	**Ver (to see/to watch)**	**Dar (to give)**	**Saber (to know)**	**Querer (to want)**
Yo	hago	veo	doy	sé	quiero
Tú	haces	ves	das	sabes	quiero
Ud./él/ella	hace	ve	da	sabe	quiere
Nosotros/as	hacemos	vemos	damos	sabemos	queremos
Vosotros/as	hacéis	veis	dais	sabéis	queréis
Uds./ellos/ellas	hacen	ven	dan	saben	quieren

Examples:

¿Qué haces? What are you doing?

Hago un sándwich. I am making a sandwich.

Veo la televisión. I am watching TV.

Vemos fútbol los domingos. We see football on Sundays.

Ellos dan el informe a José. They are giving the report to Jose.

Hoy el director da un discurso.	Today the director is giving a speech.
Yo no sé la dirección.	I don't know the address.
Sé su número de teléfono.	I know his telephone number.
¿Qué quieres tomar*?	What do you want to have?
Quiero un café.	I want a coffee.

** In Spanish language, when two verbs comes together, the first verb is conjugated and the second verb is in the infinite form which means the second verb is used without any change in its original form.*

TASKS AND EXERCISES

I. Swati is talking about herself and her family in the class. Please help her in filling the missing information from the words given below.

son	hija	está	son	tengo	llama

Me llamo Swati. ....18 años. Hay seis personas en mi familia: yo, mis padres, mis dos hermanos y mi hermana. Mi hermana se ....Sakshi y .... casada. Mis hermanos ....Rohan y Mohan. .... solteros. Sakshi tiene una .... que tiene dos años. Yo amo a mi familia.

II. A small puzzle: Guess the familial relation in each case.

1. El padre de mi madre es mi ....
2. La madre de mi esposa es mi........................
3. El hijo de la esposa de mi hermano es mi........................
4. El esposo de mi nuera es mi ....
5. La hija de mi tía es mi......................................

III. Complete the dialogues with possessive adjectives: *mi/mis, tu/tus, su/sus, nuestro/a, nuestros/nuestras, vuestro/a, vuestros/as, su/sus.*

1. Señor Wilson, ¿Me da ....bolígrafo, por favor?

   Aquí está.

2. ¿Está usted contento con ....alumnos?

   No, no son muy inteligentes.

3. ¿Dónde está vuestra casa?

   .... casa está en Delhi.

4. Hablas muy bien el alemán.

   Gracias. Es que ....madre es alemana.

5. ¿Cuál es ....número de móvil?

   Lo siento, no tengo móvil.

IV. Carmen wants to buy a gift for her mother. Complete her conversation with Pilar using the appropriate demonstrative adjectives: este/esta, ese/esa ...etc.

Carmen: Quiero comprar un libro para hacer un regalo a mi madre.

Pilar: Compramos un libro de ....librería que está aquí en frente?

Carmen: No, ...librería no tiene libros buenos. Prefiero................librería de ahí, cerca del restaurante.

Pilar: No, no me gusta esa librería porque es muy pequeña. ¿Quieres ir a.................librería de allí de la puerta verde?

Carmen: Pues, vamos allí.

THE SPANISH SPEAKING WORLD

The Hispanic family is traditionally considered to be a close-knit group. Family ties are quite strong and it is not uncommon to see people staying with their relatives and friends while travelling to another city for a short duration.

With time, the Spanish society has changed, and these days we see more and more people becoming independent. Earlier the old parents used to live with their children until death but now more and more Spaniards are placing their parents in old people's home.

In Latin America greater importance is placed on familial duty and obligation when compare to Europe. Latin American families socialise their children in family traditions and the children are expected to assist and respect the authority of the family.

CHAPTER

How to ask and tell time

Knowing to tell the time in a foreign language is an essential part of learning and it is also the most common way to break the ice in any conversation. Below you will find the basic expressions for asking and telling time in Spanish:

In Spanish the most common way to ask the time is:

¿Qué hora es? What time is it? / What´s the time?

But there are other ways of asking time which again can be classified into formal and informal ways of asking time.

Formal	
Disculpe, ¿qué hora es?	Excuse me, what time is it?
Perdone, ¿tiene hora?	Excuse me, have you got the time?
Disculpe,¿ me podría decir la hora?	Excuse me, could you please tell me the time?
Informal	
Perdona, ¿qué hora es?	Excuse me, what´s the time?
Disculpa, ¿tienes hora?	Excuse me, do you have the time?
Perdona, ¿me puedes / podrías decir la hora?	Excuse me, can /could you please tell me the time?

The typical responses to the above queries being:	
Es la una	It´s one o'clock.
Es la una **y** diez	It is ten past one. (1:10)
Son las doce **en punto**	It´s exactly twelve o´ clock.
Son las seis **menos** cuarto	It is quarter to six/ It is 5: 45
Son las siete **y** cuarto	It is quarter past seven/ It is 7: 15
Son las ocho **y media**	It is half past eight/ It is 8:30.
Son las nueve	It´s nine o´clock.
Son las once **menos** veinte	It is twenty minutes to eleven/ It is 10:40.

Below is the image of a watch with all the possible ways of telling the time in Spanish

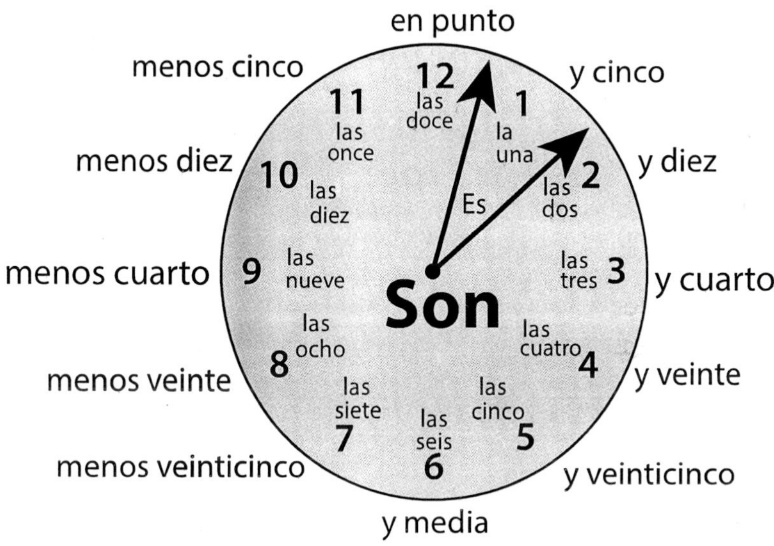

Please note that in Spanish, **son** (third person plural form of the verb **ser**) is used to tell the time. The only exception being time related to 1 o'clock as one is singular so **es** (third person singular of the verb **ser**) is used. For example: *Es la una (Its 1 o'clock) / Es la una y media (Its 1:30)/ Es la una y cuarto (Its 1:15)/ Es la una y veinte (Its 1:20)/ Es la una menos diez (Its 12:40)* etc.

While specifying the time period of the day, the following construction is used:

Son las seis **de la mañana**	It is six o clock **in the morning/** It´s 6 a.m.
Es la una **de la tarde**	It is one o ´clock **in the afternoon/** It´s 1 p.m.
Son las dos de la tarde.	It is two o ´clock in the afternoon/ It´s 2 p.m.
Son las nueve **de la noche**	It is nine o´clock **in the night**/It´s 9 p.m.
Es mediodía.	It is midday
Es medianoche	It is midnight.

Dialogue	**Diálogo**
At what time....?	***¿A qué hora.....?***
Pepe: Ms. María, at what time does the shop open?	**Pepe:** Señora María, ¿ a qué hora abre la tienda?
Ms. María: It always opens at eleven o´clock.	**Sra. María:** Abre siempre a las once.
Silvia: Carlos, at what time is the appointment?	**Silvia:** Carlos, ¿a qué hora es la cita?
Carlos: Exactly at eleven o'clock.	**Carlos:** A las once en punto.
Rosa: Excuse me, do you know at what time does the bus reach Madrid?	**Rosa:** Perdone, ¿sabe usted a qué hora llega el autobús a Madrid?
Mr. Pedro: Well, **around** eleven o' clock at night.	Don Pedro: Pues, **sobre** las once de la noche.
Peter and John in the hostel	***Pedro y Juan en la residencia***
Peter: John, what time is it?	**Pedro:** Juan,¿ qué hora es?
John: It is five o'clock.	**Juan:** Son las cinco
Peter: Oh my god! I have to meet Ana at five thirty in the cafeteria.	**Pedro:** Dios mío, tengo que ver a Ana a las cinco y media en la cafetería.

John: Well, run as it is already very late.	**Juan:** Pues, corre que ya es muy tarde.
Peter: I never reach on time. Ana is going to kill me!	**Pedro:** Nunca llego a tiempo. ¡Ana me va a matar!
John: No dude, fifteen minutes are left. You can catch the metro.	**Juan:** No tío*, quedan quince minutos. Puedes coger el metro.

* When used coloquially, tío or tía are used for referreing to friends or people of the same age group. In English, it can mean dude/ guy or gal.

VOCABULARY

La hora	Time/hour
El minuto	Minute
El segundo	Second
El reloj	Clock/ Watch
El reloj de pulsera	Wristwatch
El día	Day
La noche	Night
La semana	Week
El mes	Month
El año	Year
La semana que viene	The coming week
El mes que viene	The coming month
El año que viene	The coming year
Hoy	Today
Ayer	Yesterday
Mañana	Tomorrow
Pasado mañana	Day after tommorow

Adverbios de tiempo	**Adverbs of time**
Tarde	Late
Temprano	Early
Pronto	Soon
Normalmente	Normally
Ocasionalmente	Occassionally

Day and Date

In order to ask or tell the day and the date, you can follow the given model.

¿ Qué día es hoy?	What is the day today?
Hoy es lunes/martes/...	Today is Monday/Tuesday/...
¿ Qué día es mañana?.	What day is it tommorow?
Mañana es martes/miércoles/...	Tommorow is Tuesday/ Wednesday/...
¿ Qué fecha es hoy?	What is the date today?
Es el 2 de agosto de 2012.	It is August 2, 2012.

GRAMMAR

I. Prepositions

Prepositions in Spanish are very similar to the ones in English. Below are the most common Spanish prepositions.

A (at, to)

Llego a la oficina a las cinco.	I reach office at 5 o'clock.
Voy **al** mercado.	I am going to the market.

De (from, of)

Soy de la India.	I am from India.
Necesito una botella de agua.	I need a bottle of water.
Es el libro de Juan.	It's Juan's book.

(Literally: it is the book of Juan).

De...........a (from............to)

Trabajo de 9 a 12.	I work from 9 to 12.

Desde....................hasta (from ....till)

Trabajo desde las 9 hasta las 12.	I work from 9 till 12.

Note: While talking about time, the preposition ***de...a*** *DO NOT take definite article but* ***desde......hasta*** *TAKE definite article as seen in the examples above.*

Con (with)

Estudio con Sabrina.	I study with Sabrina.

Exception: When the preposition **con** comes with subject pronouns, then the form changes in *yo* and *tú* form:

Conmigo	Con nosotros
Contigo	Con vosotros
Con él/ella/usted	Con ellos/ ellas/usted
Eugenio: ¡Hola Juana!¿Por qué no estudias **conmigo**?	Eugenio: Hi Juana! Why don't you study **with me.**
Juana: Estudio **con Ramón** por eso no estudio **contigo.** Antonio también estudia **con nosotros.**	Juana: I study **with Ramón,** that's why I don't study **with you**. Antonio also studies **with us**.
Eugenio: ¿También puedo estudiar **con vosotros**?	Eugenio: Can I also study **with you all**?
Juana: Sí, por supuesto.	Juana: Yes, of course.

II. Adverbs of location

In English the adverbs of location are *here* and *there.*

In Spanish they are *aquí, ahí* and *allí. **Aquí(here)*** is used when the object is near the speaker, ***ahí(there)*** is used when the object is a little far from the speaker, and ***allí (there)*** is used when the object is quite far from the speaker.

III. Verb IR (to go)

The verb *Ir* means to go. It is an irregular verb which is used quite frequently when you want to say that you are going somewhere. It always take the article **a** (to). The conjugation of the verb *Ir* is given in the table below:

	IR (to go)	
Yo	voy	I go
Tú	vas	you go
Ud./él/ella	va	he/she/you go
Nosotros/as	vamos	we go
Vosotros/as	vais	you go
Uds./ellos/ellas	van	they/you go

Pedro: Hola, José. ¿ Adónde vas?.	Hi Jose. Where are you going?
Jose: Voy **a** la oficina, y ¿tú?	I am going to the office, and you?
Pedro: Voy **al** teatro.	I am going to the theatre.

Exceptions: There are some expressions used with the verb *Ir.*

Ir de compras (to go shopping)	
Hoy voy de compras con mi madre.	Today I am going shopping with my mother.
Ir de vacaciones (to go on vacation)	
El año que viene vamos de vacaciones a Barcelona.	The coming year we are going on vacation to Barcelona.

As you know, in Spanish language, when two verbs come together, the first verb is conjugated and the second verb is in the infinite form. For example:

I am going to study. In this sentence there are two verbs; to go and to study.

Voy a estudiar. So the verb *to go* is conjugated and the second verb *to study* is in the infinitive form.

You can use the other verbs that you may have learnt by now with the verb Ir. For example:

Voy a comer. — I am going to eat.

Manoj va a descansar. — Manoj is going to take rest.

Note: *Ir a + infinitive* refers to an action in future. (See Lesson 15)

TASKS AND EXERCISES

I. Tell the time of the watch given below:

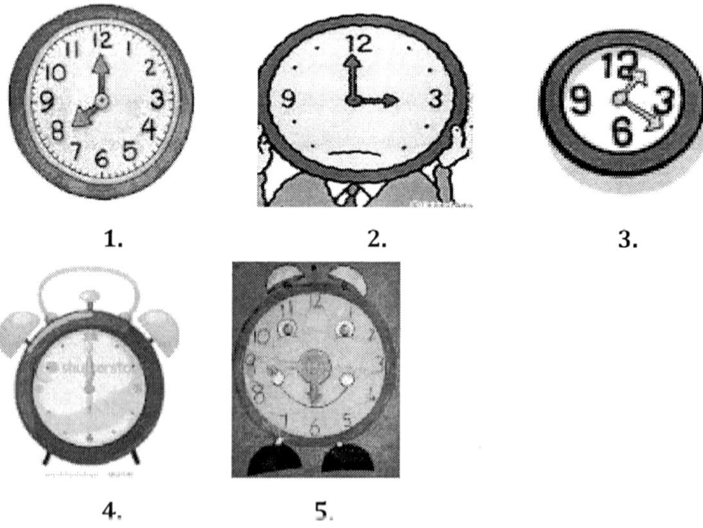

1. 2. 3. 4. 5.

II. Draw the correct time on the clock:

¿A qué hora abre la escuela?	**A las ocho menos cuarto.** 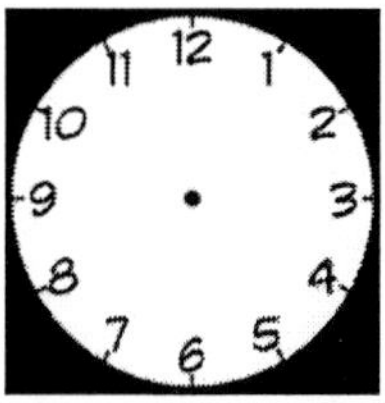
¿ A qué hora tienes el avión?	**A las seis y media.** 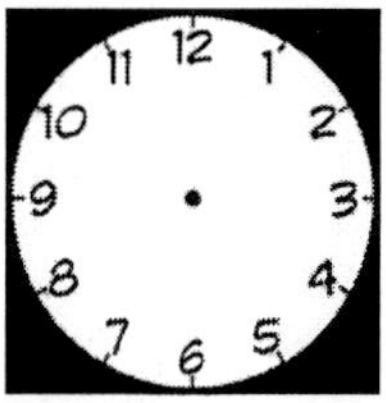
¿A qué hora sale de la universidad?	**A las cuatro y cuarto.** 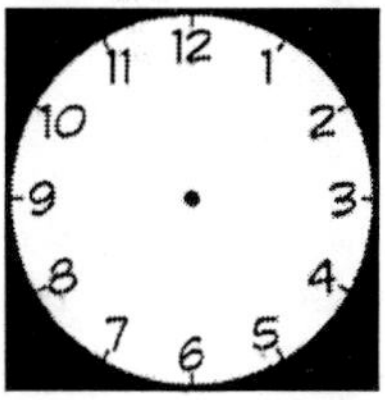
¿A qué hora vas al médico?	**A las cinco menos diez.** 
¿A qué hora llega el tren?	**A las 10 en punto.** 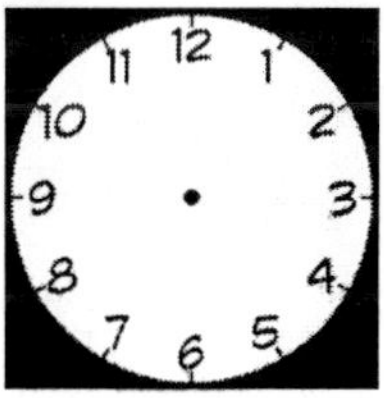

III. Fill in the blanks with the correct prepositions *a, de, con, desde, hasta.*

1. ¿ Cuántas horas trabajas?

   Trabajo ....las 9 ....las 5 de la tarde.

2. ¿Adónde vais?

   Vamos.....................supermercado.

3. ¿Con quién estudias?

   Estudio............................ Martin.

4. ¿Cuál es el horario de la oficina?

   .... 10 ....5.

THE SPANISH SPEAKING WORLD

Time difference between India and some of the Spanish speaking countries of the world is given below.

Spain	– 4:30 hours
Colombia	– 10:30 hours
Argentina	– 8:30 hours
Peru	– 10:30 hours
Mexico	– 11:30 hours
Chile	– 8:30 hours

While travelling to Spain or some other Latin American countries in summer, one has to keep in mind the day light saving time. In order to achieve longer evening daylight in summer, the time is adjusted and put one hour ahead of the standard time.

CHAPTER

Daily routine

We all follow a routine in our lives. The routine varies from country to country. Knowing to talk about what we do in our daily lives might help us, on one hand, to know about the lives of other people and on the other, to understand their culture.

Let´s see below what is the daily routine of our friend Pedro:

Pedro se levanta a las nueve de la mañana.

Pedro wakes up at 9 o´clock in the morning.

Después se lava los dientes.

Then he brushes his teeth

Se baña.

He takes a bath.

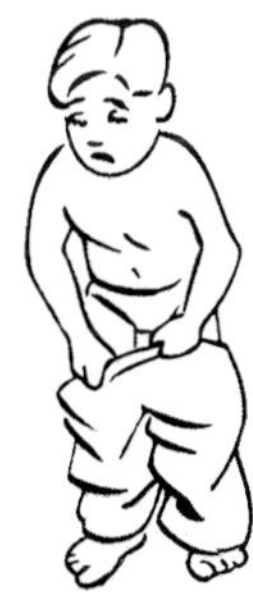

Se viste

He gets dressed

Se peina

He combs his hair.

Sale de casa a las 10.

He leaves the house at 10.

Trabaja en la oficina hasta las 8.

He works in the office till 8.

Vuelve a casa a las 9.

He returns home at 9.

Luego ve la tele

Then he watches television

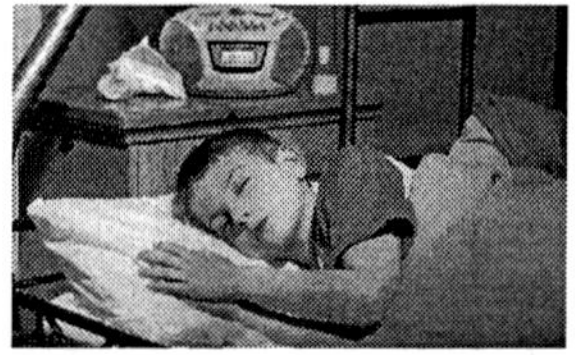

Se acuesta a las 11.

He goes to bed at 11.

As you can see in the pictures above, there are some verbs which have a 'se' preceding them like 'se peina', 'se acuesta', 'se ducha'. These verbs are known as reflexive verbs.

Dialogue:	**Diálogo:**
Antonia and Sofía meet at the school.	***Antonia y Sofía se encuentran en el colegio:***
Sofía: Antonia, you always get good grades in class. How many hours do you study every day?	**Sofía:** Antonia, siempre sacas buenas notas en clase. ¿Cuántas horas estudias cada día?
Antonia: I study for two hours before coming to the school and two hours before having dinner.	**Antonia:** Estudio dos horas antes de venir al colegio y dos horas antes de cenar.
Sofia: Are you serious? At what time do you get up?	**Sofía:** ¿En serio? A qué hora te levantas?
Antonia: I get up at six in the morning. I take a shower and take breakfast till seven o'clock. I study for two hours and then I dress up and come to the school.	**Antonia:** Me levanto a las seis de la mañana. Me ducho y desayuno hasta las siete. Estudio dos horas y luego me visto y vengo al colegio.
Sofía: And, what do you do when you go back home?	**Sofía:** Y ¿qué haces cuando vuelves a casa?

Antonia: I have snacks, I rest for a while, speak to my friends on my mobile mean while my mother prepares dinner for me. After having dinner, I do the homework and study for two hours. I go to bed at eleven o´clock.	**Antonia:** Tomo la merienda, descanso un rato, hablo con mis amigos por el móvil miencras mi madre me prepara la cena. Después de cenar, hago las tareas y estudio dos horas. Me acuesto a las 11.
Sofia: Your routine is so good!	**Sofía:** ¡Qué buena es tu rutina!

VOCABULARY

La rutina diaria	Daily routine
La oficina	Office
El baño	Bathroon
La habitación	Room
El desayuno	Breakfast
El almuerzo	Lunch
La cena	Dinner
La cama	Bed
El periódico	Newspaper
Primero	First
Luego	Later
Entonces	Then
Siempre	Always
Nunca	Never
Después	Afterwards
Antes	Before
Alm**o**rzar (ue)	To have lunch
¿A qué hora almuerzas?	At what time do you have lunch?
Almuerzo a la/las....	I have lunch at ......
Salir	To go out/ to leave
Tomar	To take
Regresar	To return
Ver la tele	To watch television

Cenar	To have dinner
Dormir (ue)	To sleep
¿ A qué hora duermes?	At what time do you sleep?
Duermo a las once.	I sleep at 11 o´clock.

GRAMMAR

In Spanish language, some verbs are reflexive and have a reflexive pronoun attached. For example, to get up early (levantarse), to wash oneself (lavarse) etc.

I. Reflexive verbs

	Levantarse (to get up)	
Yo	**me** levanto	I get up
Tú	**te** levantas	you get up
Él/ella/usted	**se** levanta	he/she/you get up
Nosotros/as	**nos** levantamos	we get up
Vosotros/as	**os** levantáis	you get up
Ellos/ellas/ustedes	**se** levantan	they get up/you get up

Examples:

(Yo) Me levanto a las ocho.	I get up at 8 o'clock.
(Ella) Se levanta temprano.	She gets up early.

	Lavarse (to wash oneself)	
Yo	me lavo	I wash (myself)
Tú	te lavas	you wash (yourself)
Él Ella Usted	se lava	he washes (himself) she washes (herself) you wash (yourself)
Nosotros/as	nos lavamos	we wash (ourselves)
Vosotros/as	os laváis	you wash (yourselves)
Ellos/ellas Ustedes	se lavan	they wash (themselves) You wash (yourselves)

Examples:

(Nosotros) Nos lavamos.	We wash ourselves.

The verb *lavar* means to wash. It can also be used as ordinary verb when the person who is doing the action is not the same person who is receiving the action. See the difference in the examples given below:

Lavo la camisa. I am washing the shirt.

Me lavo. I wash (myself)

Me lavo las manos*. I wash my hands.

* When you want to say that you are washing your body parts, the verb *lavarse* is always used. In English myself, himself, herself etc are very rarely translated. One generally says *he gets dressed* instead of saying *he dresses himself.*

Reflexive verbs can be regular or irregular. Given below are some irregular verbs.

	Despertarse (to wake up)	**Vestirse (to get dressed)**	**Acostarse (to go to bed)**
Yo	me despierto	me visto	me acuesto
Tú	te despiertas	te vistes	te acuestas
Él/ella/usted	se despierta	se viste	se acuesta
Nosotros/as	nos despertamos	nos vesti-mos	nos acostamos
Vosotros/as	os despertáis	os vestís	os acostáis
Ellos/ellas/ustedes	se despiertan	se visten	se acostan

Examples:

Me despierto a las 7. I get up at 7 o'clock.

Entonces me visto. Then I get dressed.

Me acuesto a las 11. I go to bed at 11 o'clock.

Other reflexive verbs:

afeitarse (to shave)

Él se afeita todos los días. He shaves daily.

bañarse (to take bath)

Me baño por la mañana. I take bath in the morning.

ducharse (to take shower)

¿Cuándo te duchas? When do you have shower?

enfadarse (to get angry)

Mi hermano se enfada mucho. My brother often gets angry

sentarse (to sit down)

¿Por qué no se sienta usted?. Why don't you sit down?

irse (to leave)

Me voy ahora. I am leaving now.

Note: When the verb *Ir* is used normally it means *to go*, but when it is used as a reflexive verb *Irse* it means *to leave (a place)*.

Nos vamos de aquí. We are going from here.

Me voy de vacaciones. I am leaving for vacations.

TASKS AND EXERCISES

I. Please complete the crossword puzzle below with the appropriate verbs.

Across:

1. to wash onself
3. to go
4. to have breakfast
6. to take shower
8. to go to bed
10. to wake up

Down:

2. to get up
5. to shave
7. to go out
9. to return

II. Comment on what each person is doing:

¿Qué hace Manolo?

¿Qué hace Javier?

¿Qué hace el bebé?

¿Qué hace Sebastián?

III. Match the following sentences:

1. ¿A qué hora te despiertas?	A. Veo la televisión.
2. ¿Desayunas primero o te duchas?	B. Me visto.
3. ¿Qué haces después de ducharte?	C. Duermo muy tarde.
4. ¿Qué haces antes de acostarte?	D. A las ocho y media.
5. ¿Cuándo duermes?	E. Primero me ducho y luego desayuno.

IV. You already know how to talk about your daily routine. Can you write about your daily routine below using the verbs that you know?

Me despierto a las seis y media. Luego........................

THE SPANISH SPEAKING WORLD

Daily life in Spain is not very different than the other European countries but there are some practices which are peculiar to Spain. For example:

Siesta

The *siesta* is one of the most important aspects of Spanish culture. Siesta is an afternoon nap which Spanish people take between 2 pm to 4 pm. Generally the shops are closed during this period. In today's modern globalized world, the tradition of *siesta* is declining in Spain but still it forms an important part of the way of life in smaller towns and villages.

Merienda

Merienda is the light meal taken between lunch and dinner. It generally consists of a yogurt, fruit and cookies with beverages like juice or coffee. It is necessary because of the time gap between lunch and dinner as it is customary to finish lunch by 3:30 pm and the dinner timings usually extend up to 11 pm at night.

CHAPTER

Leisure activities

Apart from the daily routine we follow, there are many activities that we do in our free time. They can be leisure activities, our hobbies or pastimes. In Spanish they can be called *actividades de ocio / aficiones / pasatiempos.*

Do you know what the verb *Gustar* means? The pictures given below will help you.

Me gusta cantar.

Me gustan las películas.

In order to say you like something, or someone, or you like doing something, in Spanish we use the verb *Gustar.*

Dialogue:	**Diálogo:**
Below, Antonio and Zara are talking about their hobbies.	***A continuación, Antonio y Zara hablan de sus aficiones.***
Antonio: Hi Zara! Where are you going?	**Antonio:** ¡Hola Zara! ¿Adónde vas?
Zara: I am going to play tennis.	**Zara:** Voy a jugar al tenis.
Antonio: How many times a week do you play?	**Antonio:** ¿Cuántas veces a la semana juegas?
Zara: Twice a week. On Mondays and Wednesdays.	**Zara:** Dos veces a la semana. Los lunes y los miércoles.
Antonio: What do you do on weekends then?	**Antonio:** ¿Qué haces los fines de semana?

Zara: On weekends, I like to hang out with my friends. Sometimes I go to the movies.	**Zara:** Los fines de semana me gusta quedar con mis amigos. A veces voy al cine.
Antonio: Well, I like to relax on weekends. Normally, on Sunday mornings, I exercise and then I surf the internet, listen to music and watch television.	**Antonio:** Pues, me gusta relajar los fines de semana. Normalmente, los domingos por la mañana hago gimnasia y luego navego por internet, escucho música y veo la tele.
Zara: Don´t you go out? How boring!	**Zara:** ¿No sales? ¡Qué aburrido!

VOCABULARY

¿Lees novelas?	Do you read novels?
Leo novelas.	I read novels.
Jugar	To play (any game)
Hacer deportes	To play sports
Tocar	To play (any musical instrument), to touch
Ir al cine	To go to the movies
Ver películas	To watch movies
Viajar	To travel
Quedar con amigos	To hang out with friends
Navegar por la red	To surf the Internet
Bailar	To dance
Cantar	To sing
Correr	To run
Escuchar la música	To listen to music
Hacer gimnasia/ ejercicios	To do exercise
Esquiar	To ski
Nadar	To swim

GRAMMAR

I. The verb Gustar and some other pronominal verbs.

The verb *Gustar* is different from other verbs as we generally use it in only two forms: ***gusta*** and ***gustan.*** It is preceded with the pronouns **me, te, le, nos, os, les** depending on the person who likes the object.

The *gusta* form is used with a singular noun.

(A mí) **Me gusta** la universidad.	**I like** the university.
(A ti) **Te gusta** el reloj.	**You like** the watch.
(A él / a ella / a usted) **Le gusta** el libro.	**He/she/you likes/ like** the book.
(A nosotros/ a nosotras) **Nos gusta** la ciudad.	**We like** the city.
(A vosotros / a vosotras) **Os gusta** la casa.	**You like** the house.
(A ellos/ a ellas/ a ustedes) **Les gusta** el hotel.	**They/you all like** the hotel.

The *gusta* form is also used with a verb. In Spanish when two verbs come together the second verb is not conjugated.

(A mi) **Me gusta** comer.	I like eating.
(A ti) **Te gusta** viajar.	You like travelling.
(A él/ a ella/ a usted) **Le gusta** ver películas.	He/she/you likes/like watching movies.
(A nosotros/ a nosotras) **Nos gusta** leer libros.	We like reading books.
(A vosotros / a vosotras) **Os gusta** nadar.	You like to swim.
(A ellos/ a ellas/ a ustedes) **Les gusta** bailar.	They/you like to dance.

The *gustan* form is used with a plural noun.

(A mí) **Me gustan** los chocolates	I like chocolates.
(A ti) **Te gustan** los relojes.	You like watches.

(A él/a ella/a usted) **Le gustan** los libros.	He/she/you likes/like books.
(A nosotros/a nosotras) **Nos gustan** las ciudades.	We like cities.
(A vosotros/a vosotras) **Os gustan** las casas.	You like the houses.
(A ellos/a ellas/a ustedes) **Les gustan** los hoteles.	They/you like the hotels.

Note: The prepositional phrase *a mí, a ti, a él, a ella, a usted, a nosotros/as, a vosotros/as, a ellos, a ellas, a ustedes* is used to remove ambiguity or add emphasis. When you say *me gusta la universidad*, **it can only mean** *I like the university*. So here the prepositional phrase *a mí* adds emphasis. But the third person singular **le** can be confusing as it can be a él / a ella / a usted/ a Juan/ a María etc, thus it becomes necessary to clarify it by adding the prepositional phrase. For example:

A usted le gusta la ciudad.	You like the city.
A María le gusta la ciudad.	Maria likes the city.

Likewise, the third person plural **les** can be for a ellos/ a ellas/ a ustedes/ a mis padres/ a mis hermanos etc, thus it become necessary to clarify it by adding the prepositional phrase.

A mis padres les gusta descansar.	My parents like to take rest.
A ellos les gustan los chocolates.	They like chocolates.

Note: It would be wrong if you say *me gusto la universidad*.

In order to say you don't like something, just add "No" before a sentence.

No me gusta comer en casa.	I don't like to eat at home.
A mis padres no les gusta descansar.	My parents don't like to take rest.
A ellos no les gustan los chocolates.	They don't like chocolates.

Note: In order to say that you hate something, use the verb "odiar".

Odio......	I hate.......
Odio trabajar.	I hate working.
Odio esta ciudad.	I hate this city.

Verbs similar to gustar:

There are other verbs which are used in the same way as the verb *gustar* that you have just learnt.

Doler* (duele, duelen) – to hurt

Me **duele** el estómago/ la cabeza.	I am having a stomach ache/ headache.
Me **duelen** los ojos.	My eyes are hurting.

*The verb *doler* is used when you want to say if any body part is hurting/aching.

Encantar (encanta, encantan)- to love something

Me encanta la pizza.	I love Pizza.
Me encantan los chocolates.	I love chocolates.

Interesar (interesa, interesan) to be of interest/interested in

Me interesa la política.	I am interested in politics.
Me interesan las novelas.	I am interested in novels.

II. More irregular verbs *Salir, Venir* and *Decir*

	Salir (to go out/ to leave)	Venir (to come)	Decir (to say)
Yo	salgo	vengo	digo
Tú	sales	vienes	dices
él/ella/usted	sale	viene	dice
Nosotros/as	salimos	venimos	decimos
Vosotros/as	salís	venís	decís
Ellos/ellas/ustedes	salen	vienen	dicen

Examples:

¿A qué hora sales?	At what time do you leave?
Salgo a las 10 de la mañana.	I leave at 10 o´clock in the morning.
¿Cuándo viene ella?	When does she come?
Ella viene a las 5 de la tarde.	She comes at 5 in the afternoon.
¿Qué dices?	What do you say?
Digo la verdad.	I say the truth.

III. The two verbs **jugar** and **tocar** mean the same – to play. The difference is that the verb **jugar** is used to play any sport and it takes the preposition ***a,*** meanwhile **tocar** is used to play any musical instrument.

	Jugar (to play any sport)	**Tocar (to play musical instruments)**
Yo	juego	toco
Tú	juegas	tocas
Él/ella/usted	juega	toca
Nosotros/as	jugamos	tocamos
Vosotros/as	jugáis	tocáis
Ellos/ellas/ustedes	juegan	tocan

Examples:

Juego al críquet.	I play cricket.
Jugamos al fútbol.	We play football.
Toco la guitarra.	I play guitar.
Tocamos el piano.	We play piano.

IV. Adverbs of frequency

The adverbs of frequency help us to specify exactly how often we do any action. It is common to hear questions like; how often do you chat with your friends? *Always, Never, Sometimes, Often* etc. Some of the most common adverbs of frequency are given below with examples.

Siempre (Always)

Siempre vamos a McDonald's.	We always go to McDonald's.

Nunca (Never)

Nunca trabajo los domingos.	I never work on Sundays.

De vez en cuando (occasionally, from time to time)

De vez en cuando visito a mis parientes.	Occasionally I visit my relatives.

A menudo (often)

A menudo como fuera.	I often eat outside.

A veces (sometimes)

A ves escucho la música.	Sometimes I listen to music.

Muchas veces (many times)

El maestro repite la frase muchas veces.	The teacher repeats the sentence many times.

Todos los días/ domingos/meses/años (every day/ Sunday/ month/year)

Todos los días estudio por la noche.	Every day I study at night.

Todas las noches/ semanas (every night/ week)

Todas las noches toco la guitarra.	Every night I play guitar.

Cada (each/every)

Cada verano vamos a las montañas.	Every summer we go to the mountains.

TASKS AND EXERCISES

I. **How often do these people do the following activities? Use adverbs of frequency given below.**

de vez and cuando, a veces, todos los días, cada mañana/tarde/ noche/día,

una vez/dos veces/ tres veces al día / a la semana / al mes / al año, a menudo

Ej: 

Carlos hace gimnasia todos los días.

Swati.............................. Prabhat..................... Dinesh...............

Rohan.................................. Shivani...............................

II. Choose the appropriate form of the verbs.

1. Me ....estudiar mucho.
   a. gusta
   b. gustan
2. Me.......................los chocolates.
   a. gusta
   b. gustan
3. Te ....las piernas.
   a. duele
   b. duelen
4. Me ....ver la tele.
   a. encanta
   b. encantan
5. Me ....viajar.
   a. interesa
   b. interesan

III. Translate the below sentences in Spanish.

1. Do you like living in India?
2. My parents don't like surfing the Internet.
3. I like playing football.
4. In my free time I like reading novels.
5. Carlos likes chocolates.

THE SPANISH SPEAKING WORLD

Latin American and Spanish cinema

Who has not heard of Penelope Cruz, Salma Hayek, Antonio Banderas. You must also have heard of Alejandro González Iñárritu, the director of *Babel.* Latin America and Spain have a very rich tradition in terms of visual spectacles and music. Directors like Pedro Almodóvar and Alejandro Amenábar from Spain have left their mark internationally. Actors like Javier Bardem are known for their Oscar winning performances.

In the 1960s Latin America experienced a new kind of film making which was termed as "New Latin American Cinema" which had a major impact. It was an *avant garde* movement which had a strong legacy of the neo-surrealistic movement which depicted and denounced the social and political crisis in the continent. Spanish directors like Carlos Saura and Luis Buñuel are masters of their craft and their original styles of film making in the post war period became an inspiration for the directors of the subsequent generations.

Latin American and Spanish cinema has produced outstanding films which have been liked and appreciated globally.

CHAPTER

9

Weather

In our day to day lives, talking about weather is a very common way to start many conversations. It is necessary to know how to talk about the climatic conditions in a foreign language because it is a nice ice breaker and it is a general topic which affects everybody. So let´s learn how to talk about the weather in Spanish:

Temperatura: 13.6 °C
Algo nublado con neblina
Humedad: 84 %
Presión: 1022.1 HPa
Visibilidad: 8 Km
Viento: 7 Km/h Sur

Read the small paragraph given below which tells about the climate in India.

El clima de la India:

En el norte de la India, en el verano hace mucho calor pero en el otoño hace fresco. Cuando llega el invierno hace frío y las noches son muy frías. En primavera el tiempo es agradable. También llueve mucho durante los monzones y hay humedad. En el sur, el tiempo no cambia mucho.

The climate of India:

In northern India, it is very hot in summer but in autumn it's cool. When the winter comes, it is cold and the nights are very cold. In spring the weather is nice. Also, it rains a lot during the monsoon and the weather is humid. In south, the weather does not change much.

Dialogue	**Diálogo**
A telephonic conversation	***Una conversación telefónica:***
Juan: Hello	**Juan:** Diga
Adolfo: Hello Juan, Adolfo speaking from the Canaries. Is it a good time to talk or should I call later?	**Adolfo:** Hola, Juan, habla Adolfo desde las Canarias. ¿Es un buen momento para hablar o llamo más tarde?
Juan: No man, it is ok. How are you?	**Juan:** No hombre, está bien. ¿Qué tal estás?
Adolfo: Very good and how are you doing?	**Adolfo:** Muy bien y tú, cómo andas?
Juan: Great! Tell me.	**Juan:** ¡Fenomenal! Dime.
Adolfo: Look, I and my wife want to travel to Barcelona. As here it is always the same weather, I want to ask you how is the weather in Barcelona. Is it very cold?	**Adolfo:** Mira, mi mujer y yo queremos hacer un viaje a Barcelona. Como aquí el tiempo siempre es igual, te quiero preguntar, ¿cómo está el tiempo en Barcelona? ¿Hace mucho frío?
Juan: No, no, here the weather is very pleasant. Even though it´s November but it is not so cold. At night, it is cool and in the day the weather is good.	**Juan:** No, no, aquí el tiempo es agradable. Aunque estamos en noviembre pero no hace tanto frío. Por la noche hace fresco y por el día hace buen tiempo.
Adolfo: I am happy to know it. So its not necessary to carry too many warm clothes. Thanks a lot. Well, see you in Barcelona.	**Adolfo:** Me alegra saberlo. Así que no es necesario llevar mucha ropa de invierno. Muchas gracias. Pues, nos vemos en Barcelona.
Juan: I am waiting for both of you eagerly. See you soon.	**Juan:** Os espero con muchas ganas. Hasta pronto.
Adolfo: See you. Bye.	**Adolfo:** Hasta pronto. Adiós.

VOCABULARY

The seasons of the year

El verano	Summer
El otoño	Autumn
El invierno	Winter
La primavera	Spring

The months of the year

enero	January
febrero	February
marzo	March
abril	April
mayo	May
junio	June
julio	July
agosto	August
septiembre	September
octubre	October
noviembre	November
diciembre	December

Note: In Spanish, the months of the year are not capitalised as in English.

Weather expressions:

In Spanish, in order to talk about the weather the verb "hacer" is used.

¿Qué tiempo hace?	How is the weather?
Hace frío	It is cold
Hace calor	It's hot.
Hace viento.	It's windy.
Hace sol.	It's sunny.
Hace fresco.	It is cool.
Hace buen tiempo.	The weather is good.

Hace mal tiempo.	The weather is bad.
¿Qué temperatura hace hoy?	What is the temperature today?
Estamos a cuarenta y cinco grados.	We are at forty five degrees.

The verb "estar" is also used when we talk about the current weather conditions.

Está despejado	It is a clear day
Está soleado	It is sunny.
Está nublado	It is cloudy.

Some other verbs used to denote weather conditions.

Llueve	(llover)	It is raining
Nieva	(Nevar)	It is snowing
Llovizna	(lloviznar)	It is drizzling

"Hay" is also used for weather expressions.

Hay niebla	It is foggy
Hay neblina	It is misty
Hay lloviznas	It is drizzling

The verb "ser" is used to talk about the climate of the place which generally doesn't change.

Es agradable.	It is pleasant.
Es húmedo	It is humid.
Es frío	It is cold.
Es caluroso o cálido	It is warm
Es seco	It is dry

GRAMMAR

Muy and Mucho

Being a beginner, the two terms **muy (very)** and **mucho (much/ many)** can be a bit confusing. The explanation given below will help you to understand their usage.

Muy has only one form. It does not change according to the number and gender. Let's see some of the examples to understand it better:

Ella habla muy bien	She speaks very well.
Martin es un chico muy inteligente.	Martin is a very intelligent boy.
La estación de metro está muy cerca.	The metro station is very near.

Mucho (a lot, many) has four forms. It agrees with the number and gender of the noun.

	Singular	Plural
Masculine	**mucho (a lot)**	**muchos (a lot, many)**
Feminine	**mucha (a lot)**	**muchas (a lot, many)**

Hace mucho calor.	It's very hot.
Hay mucha comida en casa.	There is a lot of food at home.
Mi hermano tiene muchos amigos.	My brother has many friends.
El actor tiene muchos coches.	The actor has many cars.

Mucho can also be used as an adverb.

Ella come mucho.	She eats a lot.
Él viaja mucho.	He travels a lot.

The opposite of *mucho* is *poco* (a little, few).

Like mucho , poco can be used as an adjective (**poco, poca, pocos, pocas**)

Hace poco calor.	It´s not too hot.
Hay poca comida en casa.	There is a little food at home.
Mi hermano tiene pocos amigos.	My brother has few friends.
El actor tiene pocos coches.	The actor has few cars.

Poco can also be used as an adverb.

Ella come poco.	She eats a little.
Él viaja poco.	He travels a little.

TASKS AND EXERCISES

I. Tell the weather on the basis of the images given below.

II. Look at the weather map of India. Can you tell how the weather in several cities of India is?

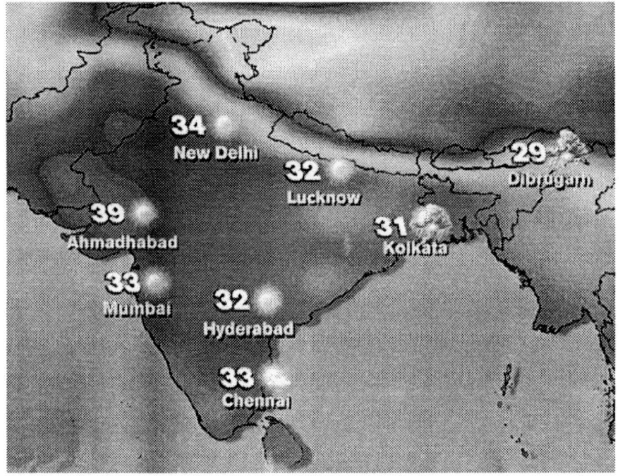

1. En Nueva Delhi, ...
2. Si vives en Kolkata, lleva paraguas porque.....................
3. En Chennai, el cielo..............................
4. En Mumbai.......................humedad.
5. En Ahmadabad estamos a 39 grados. Hace.................

III. Complete with *muy, mucho o poco:*

1. En Ladakh hace......................frío.
2. Llueve.............en Ahmedabad. Por eso el clima es ....seco.
3. Kolkata está...............cerca de Darjeeling.
4. En el invierno, en Darjeeling hay.........neblina.
5. En el monzón, llueve..............

IV. Look for the seasons and months of the year in the puzzle given below. There are eight words in total.

M	Q	V	V	E	N	E	R	O	Y	I	M	K	N	N
K	Z	O	E	F	R	N	U	O	Y	A	A	X	N	F
O	P	N	P	R	I	M	A	V	E	R	A	L	C	O
C	Ñ	N	E	E	A	R	M	Z	K	B	E	J	Y	E
I	C	O	I	K	D	N	O	E	S	N	V	P	V	D
A	Q	V	T	R	A	G	O	S	T	O	A	O	E	U
B	N	A	G	O	S	T	O	L	Q	C	M	F	R	V
R	D	A	G	Q	H	D	M	I	A	L	I	R	A	A
I	U	M	B	F	H	X	A	J	G	Z	R	D	N	N
L	S	F	H	G	W	V	Y	F	X	G	P	R	O	X
E	W	E	Q	K	Z	G	O	V	D	V	X	I	Q	O
E	I	T	I	N	V	I	E	R	N	O	E	S	O	H
O	O	M	T	M	J	I	R	H	C	R	F	F	Y	Z
E	K	U	B	D	J	O	Z	T	R	O	L	I	A	J
P	L	C	V	E	M	A	R	Z	O	W	J	I	M	N

THE SPANISH SPEAKING WORLD

Latin America boasts of a geographically very diverse landscape from the deserts of Patagonia to the world's highest mountain ranges of the Andes, from the grasslands of the Pampas to the world's largest rainforests of the Amazon, the rich and very peculiar flora and fauna and the cultural diversity of the ancient tribal population are one of its kind in the world. Did you know that potato, chocolate and tomato were all discovered in Latin America?

CHAPTER

At the airport

As you travel to a Spanish speaking country, the first encounter with Spanish happens at the airport when you land. Below you will find a list of vocabulary and expressions that will help you to manage the situation in an airport or customs. Let's look at the conversation that takes place at the ticket counter in Madrid while Sara is trying to book a ticket for Berlin.

Dialogue	**Diálogo**
In the airport:	***En el aeropuerto:***
Employee: Good morning, how can I help you?	**Empleado:** Buenos días, ¿en qué puedo servirle?
Sara: Good morning. Are there seats available in the plane that leaves now for Berlin?	**Sara:** Hola ¿hay plazas disponibles en el avión que sale ahora para Berlín?
Employee: One moment please. Yes ma´am, we have seats available.	**Empleado:** Un momento, por favor. Sí señora, tenemos disponibilidad de plazas.
Sara: How much does the ticket cost?	**Sara:** ¿Cuánto cuesta el billete?
Employee: 150 euros	**Empleado:** 150 euros.

Sara: Perfect. Can you give me a return ticket? The return is on the 2nd of November.	**Sara:** Perfecto ¿Me das un billete de ida y vuelta? La vuelta es para el 2 de noviembre.
Employee: All right, aisle or window?	**Empleado:** De acuerdo, ¿pasillo o ventanilla?
Sara: I prefer one near to the emergency exit.	**Sara:** Prefiero uno cerca de la salida de emergencia.
Employee: Ok. Your name and your passport number, please.	**Empleado:** Vale. Su nombre y su número de pasaporte, por favor.
Sara: My name is Sara Rodriguez and the passport number is K1023452.	**Sara:** Me llamo Sara Rodríguez y el número de pasaporte es K1023452.
Employee: Thanks a lot Ms. Sara. Here it is. The flight has a stopover in Paris.	**Empleado:** Muchas gracias, doña Sara. Aquí lo tiene. El vuelo hace una escala en París.
Sara: Thanks. Where do I check-in my luggage?	**Sara:** Gracias. ¿Dónde debo facturar mi equipaje?
Employee: There in the desk number 6 at the end, to the left.	**Empleado:** Ahí en el mostrador número seis al fondo a la izquierda.
Sara: Thanks a lot. Bye.	**Sara:** Muchas gracias. Adiós.

When you reach any country, the immigration officers at the airport ask you some questions and verify your passport and visa. The conversation below can serve as a model.

Your Passport please......	**Su pasaporte, por favor...**
In the customs or Passport control	***En las aduanas o control de pasaporte***
Employee: Your reason for coming to Spain?	**Empleado**: ¿Su motivo de venir a España?
Sara: I am a student and I have come to do a Spanish course in Madrid.	**Sara**: Es que soy estudiante y vengo a hacer un curso de español en Madrid.
Employee: Can you show me your passport, please. At what address you are going to stay in Madrid?	**Empleado**: Me puede enseñar su pasaporte, por favor. ¿Cuál es la dirección donde va a vivir en Madrid?
Sara: I am going to stay in a rented flat in Gibraltar Street	**Sara**: Voy a vivir en un piso alquilado en la calle Gibraltar.
Employee: For how long are you going to stay in Spain?	**Empleado**: ¿Por cuánto tiempo va a quedarse en España?
Sara: The course is of one month. So I am thinking of staying in Spain approximately for one and a half month.	**Sara**: El curso es de un mes. Así que pienso estar en España aproximadamente un mes y medio.
Employee: Do you have anything to declare?	**Empleado**: ¿Tiene algo que declarar?
Sara: No, I only have articles of personal use.	**Sara**: No, sólo tengo artículos de uso personal.
Employee: All right. Here is your passport. You can pass now. Welcome to Spain.	**Empleado**: Vale. Aquí tiene su pasaporte. Ya puede pasar. Bien venido a España.
In the airport	***En el aeropuerto***
Sara: Where is the boarding gate?	**Sara:** ¿Dónde está la puerta de embarque?
Employee: It is straight, to the right.	**Empleado:** Está todo recto, a la derecha.
Sara: Thanks a lot.	**Sara:** Muchas gracias.
Empleado: You´re welcome.	**Empleado:** De nada.

On the street	***En la calle***
Sara: Excuse me, where is the bus stop for going to the airport?	Sara: Perdone, ¿dónde está la parada de autobús para ir al aeropuerto.
Rodrigo: There it is, in front of the supermarket.	Rodrigo: Ahí está enfrente del supermercado.
In the office	***En la oficina***
Manager: Where is the ticket?	Gerente: ¿Dónde está el billete?
Secretary: In your cabin, on the table.	Secretaria: En su despacho, encima de la mesa.

VOCABULARY

El pasaporte	Passport
El aeropuerto	Airport
El billete	Ticket (bus, train , plane etc)
La entrada	Ticket (cinema, theatre etc)
El visado	Visa
La tarjeta de embarque	Boarding pass
El mostrador de facturación	Check-in desk
El equipaje de mano	Hand baggage
El control de seguridad	Security check
La llegada	Arrival
La salida	Departure
La recogida de equipaje	Baggage claim
La puerta de embarque	Boarding gate
A bordo	On board
El avión	Plane
El vuelo	Flight
El horario	Timetable
El retraso	Delay
El pasillo	Aisle
La ventanilla	Window
La cabina	Cabin

El cinturón de seguridad	Safety belt
El asiento	Seat
El auxiliar de vuelo	Stewards
La azafata	Air hostess
La tripulación	Crew
Libre de impuestos	Duty free
El/La dependiente/a	Salesman/Saleswoman
Aterrizar	To land
¿A qué hora aterriza el avión?	At what time the plane lands?
Despegar	To take off
El avión despega a las 8.	The plane takes off at 8.

GRAMMAR

I. Costar (to cost)

In order to ask the price of anything we use the verb *costar.* It has got only two forms: **cuesta** and **cuestan.**

The form **cuesta** is used with singular nouns.

¿Cuánto cuesta el billete?	How much does the ticket cost?
Cuesta doscientas rupias.	It costs two hundred rupees.
¿Cuánto cuesta la camisa?	How much does the shirt cost?
Cuesta seiscientas rupias.	It costs six hundred rupees.

The form **cuestan** is used with plural nouns.

¿Cuánto cuestan los pantalones?	How much do the trousers cost?
Cuestan cincuenta euros	They cost fifty euros.
¿Cuánto cuestan los zapatos?	How much do the shoes cost?
Cuestan dos mil trescientas rupias.	They cost two thousand and three hundred rupees.

Note: The price can be also asked by using the verb *SER or VALER.*

Examples:

¿Cuánto vale?	What is the cost?
¿Cuánto es?	What is the cost?

II. Prepositions of place

Below is a list of a few prepositions of place. They are used while asking and giving directions or location of a particular place or thing.

Dentro de / en (inside)

La pelota está dentro de/en la mochila.	The ball is in the bag.

Sobre/en (on)

La pelota está sobre/en la mesa.	The ball is on the table.

Fuera de (outside)

La pelota está fuera de la casa.	The ball is outside the house.

Detrás de (behind)

La pelota está detrás de la silla.	The ball is behind the chair.

Delante de (in front of)

La pelota está delante de la clase.	The ball is in front of the class.

Debajo de (under)

La pelota está debajo de la cama.	The ball is under the bed.

Cerca de (near)

La pelota está cerca de la bicicleta.	The ball is near the bicycle.

Lejos de (far)

La pelota está lejos de la bicicleta.	The ball is far from the bicycle.

A la izquierda (to the left)

La pelota está a la izquierda de Pedro.	The ball is to the left of Pedro.

A la derecha (to the right)

La pelota está a la derecha de María.	The ball is to the right of Maria.

TASKS AND EXERCISES

I. Match the dialogues:

1.	¿Su número de pasaporte, por favor?	A.	Ocho kilos.
2.	¿Tenéis algo que declarar?	B.	Lo siento, no las tenemos disponibles.
3.	¿Dónde podemos facturar la maleta?	C.	Ahí al fondo a la derecha.
4.	Hay plazas disponibles en el avión para Madrid?	D.	Es el K1072048
5.	Dónde están las puertas del embarque?	E.	No, sólo llevamos cosas de uso personal.
6.	Cuánto debe pesar el equipaje de mano?	F.	En el mostrador de facturación en frente.

II. ¿Dónde está................?

i. Answer the following questions:

a. ¿Dónde está la silla? ____________________

b. ¿Dónde está la pelota? ____________________

c. ¿Dónde está la lámpara? ____________________

d. ¿Dónde está el gato? ____________________

e. ¿Dónde está el jarrón de flores? ____________________

ii. **Answer *sí* or *no* and if the answer is *no* then write the correct location:**

a. ¿Está la alfombra lejos del sofá?____________________

b. ¿Está el gato detrás del sofá?____________________

c. ¿Está la silla entre la mesa y el sofá? ____________________

d. ¿Está el sofá en el centro de la habitación? ____________________

e. ¿Está el sofá a la izquierda de la mesa? ____________________

III. Imagine you are in a duty free shop at El Dorado international airport, Bogotá. You want to buy some gifts for yourself and for your friends before you take the plane back to India. You need to ask the price of each of these products as per the example given below.

Tú: ¿Cuánto cuesta esta botella de perfume?

Dependiente: $ 90.

1.

Tú: ¿..?

Dependiente: $ 110.

2.

Tú: ¿..?

Dependiente: $ 70.

Tú: ¿..?
Dependiente: $ 50.

Tú: ¿..?
Dependiente: $ 35.

THE SPANISH SPEAKING WORLD

In the year 1492, a Genovese navigator Christopher Columbus received a commission from the Spanish kings to start an expedition to find the shortest route to India in order to start trade relations with the golden bird of the east, but instead Columbus landed on the shores of a new continent and mistakenly thought that he has reached India. That's why he called the indigenous inhabitants *indios* and the continent as *Las Indias.* The new continent was already an inhabited land with highly developed civilizations. These were the Mayas, the Incas and the Aztecs. Machhu Picchu in Peru constructed by the Incas and the Mesoamerican Pyramids in Mexico are world heritage sites now.

In the hotel

When we travel to a Spanish speaking country, it is important to know how to order food in a restaurant and how to make reservation in a hotel. In this lesson, we will learn to do both.

Meals, in Spain and Latin America, generally have three courses: *el primer plato, el segundo plato* and *el postre*. The first is appetizers or starters which generally consist of salads or soups. The second is the main course where people take any kind of meat or fish. With the meal they usually order something to drink. Finally comes the dessert. After the meal it is habitual to have coffee.

They have light breakfast. The lunch is the heaviest meal of the day which one has around 2 pm to 4 pm. Dinner timings are usually from 9 pm to 10: 30 pm. In between the meals it is very habitual to take snacks (merienda). The Spanish people love to hang out in bars with their friends and have tapas which are nothing but small portion of food that one takes with the drinks.

Dialogue	**Diálogo**
In the restaurant of La Ronda hotel:	***En el restaurante del hotel la Ronda***
Mr. Rodrigo: Hello, do you have a free table?	**Sr. Rodrigo:** Hola, ¿tiene una mesa libre?
Waiter: Yes sir, there at the end, near the window.	**Camarero:** Sí señor, ahí al fondo, cerca de la ventana.
Mr. Rodrigo: Thanks. Can you bring me the menu, please?	**Sr. Rodrigo:** Gracias. ¿Me trae la carta por favor?
Waiter: Here it is. Do you know yet what are you going to order?	**Camarero:** Aquí la tiene. ¿Ya sabe qué va a pedir?
Mr. Rodrigo: Yeah, I want a vegetable soup to begin with and for the main course...I don´t know What do you recommend?	**Sr. Rodrigo:** Sí, de primero quiero una sopa de verduras y de segundo..no sé..¿qué me recomienda usted?
Waiter: Well, the Madrilenian stew is the house specialty.	**Camarero:** Pues, el cocido madrileño es la especialidad de la casa.
Mr. Rodrigo: Well, alright! The stew as main course.	**Sr. Rodrigo:** ¡Pues, muy bien! El cocido de segundo.
Waiter: Would you like some dessert?	**Camarero:** ¿Quiere algo de postre?
Mr Rodrigo: Plain yoghurt.	**Sr Rodrigo:** Yogur natural.
Waiter: And to drink, what do you want?	**Camarero:** Y para beber, ¿qué desea?
Mr Rodrigo: A beer, please.	**Sr Rodrigo:** Una cerveza, por favor.
In the reception of La Ronda hotel:	***En la recepción del hotel La Ronda:***
Mr. Rodrigo: Good Morning, do you have any room available?	**Sr. Rodrigo**: Buenos días, tienen ustedes una habitación disponible?
Recepcionista: Yes sir, for how many days you want it?	**Recepcionista:** Sí señor. ¿Por cuántos días la quiere?

Mr. Rodrigo: For one week. I want a double room.	**Sr Rodrigo:** Por una semana. Quiero una habitación doble.
Receptionist: All right. A/C or non A/C?	**Recepcionista**: De acuerdo. ¿Con aire acondicionado o sin aire acondicionado?
Mr. Rodrigo: How much does an A/ C room cost?	**Sr Rodrigo:** ¿Cuánto cuesta un cuarto con aire acondicionado?
Receptionist: 80 euros per day with breakfast included.	**Recepcionista:** 80 euros por día con desayuno incluido.
Mr Rodrigo: Well, it´s ok.	**Sr Rodrigo:** Pues, está bien.
Receptionist: Please sign the register. Here are your keys. The porter will carry your luggage to your room.	**Recepcionista:** Por favor, firme el registro. Las llaves aquí las tiene. El portero va a llevar su equipaje hasta su habitación.
Mr.Rodrigo: Thanks. Please give me a wake up call at 5 o´clock tomorrow.	**Sr. Rodrigo:** Gracias. Por favor, despiérteme mañana a las cinco.

VOCABULARY

El restaurante	**The restaurant**
Una mesa para tres, por favor.	A table for three, please.
¿Tiene platos vegetarianos?	Do you have any vegetarian dishes?
¿Dónde están los servicios?	Where are the toilets?
El bar	Bar
La cafetería	Cafeteria
La comida	Food
La comida rápida	Fast food
El menú del día	Daily special menu
El primer plato	Appetizers/ Starters
El segundo plato	Main Course
El postre	Dessert
La bebida	Drink
La cuenta	Bill

La carta	Menu Card
La propina	Tip
La servilleta	Napkin
La cuchara	Spoon
El cuchillo	Knife
El tenedor	Fork
La servilleta	Napkin
El vaso	Glass
La taza	Cup
El autoservicio	Self service
El refresco	Cold drink
El helado	Ice cream
Las tapas	Small portions of food served in bar and cafes with a drink.
El agua mineral	Mineral water
El vino	Wine
Probar (o-ue)	To taste (the food)/ To try (clothes)/ to test
Alojarse	To stay
Traer	To bring
El hotel	**Hotel**
Quiero hacer una reserva en su hotel	I want to make a reservation in your hotel
El hotel	Hotel
El alojamiento	Lodging
La pensión/Elhostal	Boarding house
El albergue juvenil	Youth hostel
La habitación doble	Double room
La habitación individual	Single room
La suite	Suite
La cama individual	Single bed
La cama de matrimonio	Double bed

La habitación privada	Room with bathroom attached
La recepción	Reception
El servicio de lavandería	Laundry service

GRAMMAR

1. Object Pronouns:

A pronoun is a word that takes the place of a noun. It replaces the noun when it is clear what or whom we are talking about. There are two types of object pronouns: direct and indirect. For example:

Ram gave the pen to Maria.

In the above sentence you have two objects: *the pen* and *Maria*. The action of the verb falls directly on *the pen* therefore it is the direct object. It is what was given. The action of the verb falls indirectly on Maria; it is to whom it was given, therefore *Maria* is the indirect object.

a. Complemento Directo/Direct Object

Direct object pronouns are, me, him, you, us and them and it generally comes before the verb.

Complemento Directo	Direct object
me	me
te	you
lo(masculine) la (feminine)	him/it (masculine) you(formal) her/it(feminine)
nos	us
os	you
los(masculine) las (feminine)	them(masculine)/ you (plural formal) them (feminine)

Te veo.	I see you
Os quiero.	I love you all.
Ella **nos** ayuda con la carta.	She helps us with the letter.

b. Complemento indirecto/Indirect object

The object on which the action of the verb falls indirectly is called indirect object.

Complemento indirecto	Indirect object
me	to me
te	to you (familiar)
le	to him, to her, to you(formal), to it.
nos	to us
os	to you (familiar plural)
les	to them, to you(formal plural)

Indirect object pronouns are the same for masculine and feminine. For example, *le* is used for both "to him" and "to her".

Te doy un regalo.	I give you a gift. (I give a gift to you)
Le digo la verdad.	I tell him/her the truth. (I tell the truth to you)
Él no **me** escribe ninguna carta.	He doesn´t write any letter to me.
¿**Nos** sirves la comida?	Are you serving the food to us?
La profesora **les** explica bien la lección.	The professor explains the lesson well to them.

II. The Prepositions 'Por' and 'Para'

The prepositions *para* and *por* can be a bit confusing for a Spanish learner as both can mean *for*. One understands it better only with practice.

Para

1. Means *for* when used with a *person, purpose* or *destination.*

El regalo es para mi madre.	The gift is for my mother.
Para mí, un café por favor.	For me one coffee please.
La taza es para leche.	The cup is for milk.
Salgo para Delhi.	I am leaving for Delhi.

2. Means *in order to* when used with a verb.

Para ir a España, tienes que comprar el billete	In order to go to Spain, you have to buy the ticket.

Por

1. Means *for* when used with expressions of *exchange, while expressing gratitude and to denote something happening over a fixed period of time.*

Te doy diez rupias por la pluma.	I give you 10 rupees for the pen.
Gracias por la ayuda.	Thanks for the help.
Estudio por dos horas cada día.	I study for two hours every day.

2. Means *in* when used for *time.*

Por la mañana (in the morning)

Desayuno por la mañana.	I have breakfast in the morning.

Por la tarde (in the afternoon)

Trabajo por la tarde.	I work in the afternoon.

Por la noche (at night)

Veo la televisión por la noche.	I watch television at night.

TASKS AND EXERCISES

I. Put the following dialogues in the correct order:

__ ¿Y algo de beber?

__ ¿Y de segundo que desea?

__ De segundo pollo con champiñones.

__ Hola, ¿qué desea comer?.

__ De primero quiero una ensalada mixta.

__ Muy bien ¿Desea algo de postre?

__ Pues, me trae una botella de vino por favor.

__ Enseguida.

__ Sí, una tarta de queso.

II. Complete the dialogue with the appropriate direct and indirect object pronoun:

Juan and Silvia in a bar:

Camarero: Hola ¿Qué ..... pongo?

Juan y Silvia: .... pone un café y una coca cola por favor.

Camarero: ¿Desea algo de comer?

Silvia y Juan: Es que somos turistas. No sabemos qué tienen para comer.

Camarero: Pues, tenemos tapas de gambas, queso, tortilla y champiñones. Además tenemos tarta de queso y flan.

Juan: No sé...¿qué .... recomienda usted de tapas?

Camarero: Bueno, ... recomiendo tapas de champiñones y de tortilla de patatas. Están buenas.

Silvia: También........... trae una de queso por favor. Me gusta mucho.

Camarero: Enseguida.

Silvia y Juan: Gracias.

III. Fill in the blanks using *por* or *para*.

1. La habitación es ....mi padre.
2. Voy a comer en el restaurante del hotel................ la tarde.
3. La habitación cuesta mil rupias.................día.
4. ¿................cuántos días quiere quedarse en nuestro hotel?
5. Necesita un taxi............................ir al hotel.

THE SPANISH SPEAKING WORLD

Gastronomy

Drinking wine and beer with food is normal in Spain and Latin America.

Tapas are small portion of prepared food which are generally served in bars and cafés. Some of the common tapas are Spanish omelette, seafood, olives etc.

As the people in Spain have dinner after 9 pm, it is very common to go to bar which are open all day long till late at night and have tapas. There is an expression in Spanish which is *Ir de tapas* (Bar hopping) as going for tapas is very popular.

Paella is a much known dish of Spain. It is made of rice, meat, seafood and vegetables. The paella of Valencia is the most famous.

Gazpacho is a kind of cold soup made of cucumber, garlic and tomatoes.

If we talk about Latin America, its rich cultural diversity and links with the Mesoamerican culture of the past have produced a rich fusion cuisine. Mexican cuisine is world known for its rich combination of flavours. Quesadilla, Mexican tortilla, tacos, burritos are examples of some of the well known Mexican dishes. Mexico is also famous for its tequila and likewise down south, Chilean wines are making huge impact these days.

CHAPTER

12 To go shopping

People in general love shopping. Spain is famous for its popular clothing brands like *Zara* and *Mango* and many others. As usual there is a huge rush during the sales (*las rebajas)* which happen in July end till September beginning, and after January 6 till February end. In this lesson you will find some useful expressions which will help you while shopping in the Hispanic world.

¿Qué desea(n)?	What do you wish for?
Quería/ Quiero ...	I wanted/ I want....
¿Qué talla usa(n)? / ¿De qué talla?	What size do you wear/ of which size?
La 36/ La S	36/ S
¿Tiene una talla más/menos grande?	Do you have this in larger/ smaller size
¿De qué color es .....?	What is the color of....?
Rojo/ negro...........	Red/ Black.....
¿Cómo me queda? / ¿Qué tal me queda?	How does it look on me?/ How does it fit me?
Te queda bien/ perfecto/ grande/ estrecha/ mal....	It looks good/perfect/ big/ tight/ bad on you...
¿Cuál prefieres?	Which one do you prefer?

Prefiero la roja/ el negro/ la de algodón/ el de lana.....	I prefer the red one/ the black one/ the cotton one/ the woollen one.
¿Qué te parece?	What do you think of it?
Me parece perfecto/ bien/ bonito/ barato/ caro	I find it perfect/ good/ beautiful/ cheap/ expensive
¿Cuál te gusta(n) más/ menos?	Which one do you like the most/ the least?
Me gusta(n) los rojos/ el negro/ el de lana/ la de piel..	I like the red ones/ the black one/ the woollen one/ the leather one.
¿Cuánto es?	¿How much is it?
Son 60 rupias	It is 60 rupees
¿Cuánto cuesta(n)?	¿How much does it/ do they cost?
Cuesta(n) 100 rupias	It costs/ they cost 100 rupees.
Son de temporada. No están en oferta	They are from the new collection. They are not on sale.
¿Me lo puedo probar?	Can I try it?

Dialogue	**Diálogo**
In a shop.	***En una tienda.***
Saleswoman: Good morning, how may I help you?	**Dependienta:** Buenos días ¿En qué le puedo servir?
Customer: Hello, I want to buy a t-shirt for myself.	**Cliente:** Hola, quiero comprar una camiseta para mí.
Saleswoman: What size do you wear?	**Dependienta:** ¿Qué talla lleva?
Customer: 42	**Cliente:** La 42
Customer: Here all are of cotton. Do you have them in silk also?	**Cliente:** Aquí son todas de algodón. ¿Las tienen de seda también?
Saleswoman: Yes, they are there near the mirror.	**Dependienta:** Sí, están allí cerca del espejo.

Customer: I really like the design of this one. Do you have it in another color? Actually, red does not suit me.	**Cliente:** Me gusta mucho el diseño de ésta. ¿La tiene usted en otro color? Es que el rojo no me queda bien.
Saleswoman: Yes, we have them in three more colors.	**Dependienta:** Sí, las tenemos en tres colores más.
Customer: Oh, I love the blue one! It's very cute. How much does it cost?	**Cliente:** Ay, ¡Me encanta la azul! Es muy linda. ¿Cuánto cuesta?
Saleswoman: 49.50 euros only.	**Dependienta:** Sólo 49,50 euros.
Customer: How expensive! Don´t you have other cheaper ones?	**Cliente:** ¡Qué cara! ¿No tiene otras más baratas?
Saleswoman: No, in this design and in this size we only have these.	**Dependienta:** No, en este diseño y en esta talla sólo tenemos éstas.
Customer: Can I try it?	**Cliente:** ¿Me la puedo probar?
Saleswoman: Yes, the trial rooms are at the end to the right	**Dependienta:** Sí, los probadores están al fondo a la derecha. .....
Saleswoman: How does it fit you?	**Dependienta:** ¿Qué tal le queda?
Customer: It fits perfect. I'll take it.	**Clienta:** Me queda perfecto. Me la llevo.
Cashier: How do you want to pay? By card or in cash?	**Cajera:** ¿Cómo quiere pagar, con tarjeta o en efectivo?
Customer: By card.	**Cliente:** Con tarjeta.
Cashier: Here is your purchase and your receipt.	**Cajera:** Aquí tiene su compra y su ticket de compra.
Customer: Thank you.	**Cliente:** Gracias.
Cashier: Thanks to you. See you later.	**Cajera:** A usted. Hasta luego.

VOCABULARY

Los colores	**Colors**
Amarillo	Yellow
Naranja	Orange
Azul	Blue
Blanco	White

Dorado	Golden
Gris	Grey
Marrón	Brown
Negro	Black
Morado	Purple
Rojo	Red
Rosa	Pink
Verde	Green

In Spanish the colors follow the number and gender of the noun. In order to ask the color, you have to ask **¿De qué color es?** or **¿De qué color son?.**

¿De qué color es **la chaqueta**?	What colour is the jacket?
Es azul	It´s blue.
¿De qué color son **los zapatos**?	What colour are the shoes?
Son negros.	They are black.

Ir de compras	**To go shopping**
La tienda	Shop
El supermercado	Supermarket
El centro comercial	Shopping centre
La joyería	Jewellery store
La frutería	Fruit store or shop
La librería	Book store
La peluquería	Hairdressing salon
La zapatería	Shoe shop
La papelería	Stationary store
El cajero automático	ATM
La tarjeta de débito	Debit card
La tarjeta de crédito	Credit card

La ropa	**Clothes**
La camisa	Shirt
La camiseta	T-shirt
La blusa	Blouse
Los pantalones	Trousers
Los pantalones cortos	Shorts / short pants

La falda	Skirt
Los vaqueros	Denim/Jeans
El sombrero	Hat
La corbata	Tie
La gorra	Cap
La chaqueta	Jacket
La sudadera	Sweatshirt
El jersey	Jersey
El pañuelo	Handkerchief
La bufanda	Scarf
Los guantes	Gloves
Las medias	Stockings
Los calcetines	Socks
Los zapatos	Shoes
Las zapatillas	Slippers
Las zapatillas de deporte	Sports shoes
Las sandalias	Scandal
La talla	Size

Materiales	**Materials**
Es de seda/ algodón	It's of silk / cotton
El algodón	Cotton
La seda	Silk
La lana	Wool
El lino	Linen
El nilón	Nylon

Verbos	**Verbs**
Regatear	To bargain
Comprar	To purchase
Vender	To sell
Regalar	To gift

GRAMMAR

1. Comparatives and superlatives of Adjectives

In English in order to compare things we use **more (más)** or **less (menos)** before the adjective or **'er'** at the end of the adjective. For example: *more intelligent, less rich, cheaper.*

The superlatives are the one where we use **most (el/la más)** or **least (el/la menos)** in front of the adjectives or **'est'** at the end of the adjectives. For example: *most intelligent, least rich, cheapest.* The superlatives can be differentiated from the comparative as it **uses the definite article** in Spanish.

Adjective	**Comparative**	**Superlative**
inteligente (intelligent)	más inteligente (more intelligent)	el más inteligente (the most inteligent).
	menos inteligente (less intelligent)	el menos inteligente (the least intelligent)
rico (rich)	más rico (richer)	el más inteligente (the richest)
	menos rico (less rich)	el menos rico (the least rich)
barato(cheap)	más barato (cheaper)	el más barato (the cheapest)
	menos rico (less cheap)	el menos rico (the least cheap)

In Spanish, the comparative uses más (more), menos (less) before the adjectives. See the examples with **más (more).**

Ella es más inteligente.	She is more intelligent.
Él es más rico.	He is richer
Esta camisa es más barata.	This shirt is cheaper.

In order to make comparison with anyone or anything else **que** (than) is used.

Ella es más inteligente que él.	She is more intelligent than him.
Él es más rico que su hermano.	He is richer than his brother.

Esta camisa es más barata que ésa.	This shirt is cheaper than that one.

The superlatives are used with the definite article **el/la los/las**.

Ella es la más inteligente.	She is the most intelligent.
Él es el más rico.	He is the richest.
Esta camisa es la más barata.	This shirt is the cheapest.

For superlatives with a noun use the construction el/la los/las + noun + más/menos + adjective.

Es la corbata más cara que tenemos.	It is the most expensive tie that we have.
Son los hoteles más baratos de la ciudad.	They are the cheapest hotels of the city.
Es la camisa menos cara.	It is the cheapest shirt.

Note: Although all the adjectives can be compared as per the rule mentioned above, there are some exceptions.

Adjective	**Comparative**	**Superlative**
bueno (good)	mejor (better)	el mejor (the best)
malo (bad)	peor (worse)	el peor (the worst)
gande (big)	mayor (elder)	el mayor (the eldest)
pequeño (small)	menor (younger)	el menor (the youngest)

Es el mejor.	It is the best.
Es el peor.	It is the worst.
Es mi hermano mayor.	He is my elder brother.
Es mi hermana menor.	She is my younger sister.
Soy el mayor de mis hermanos.	I am the oldest of my brothers.

2. Comparison of equality.

When we have to compare two equal things, we use:

a. tan.............como (as .... as).

Ranjeet es tan alto como Rakesh.	Ranjeet is as tall as Rakesh.
Ramneek as tan guapa como Pooja.	Ramneek is as pretty as Pooja.

b. tanto/a tantos/as .... como (as many ....as).

Tengo tantos coches como mi amigo.	I have as many cars as my friend.

Mi madre lee tantas novelas como yo.	My mother reads as many novels as I.

TASKS AND EXERCISES

I. Use the sentences and questions given in the box and fill in the blanks.

1. ¿ En qué le puedo ayudar?
   - ....
2. ¿ ....?
   - La 40.
3. ¿Cuál de las dos camisas te gustan más?
   - ....
4. Esta camisa me parece linda.

   ¿ ....?
   - Claro, los probadores están al fondo.
5. ¿Cómo quiere pagar?
   - ....

-¿Qué talla de camisa lleva?
-Con tarjeta.
-Quiero comprar una camisa negra.
-La roja.
- Me la puedo probar

II. Look at the pictures and write how are they called in Spanish.

1 .... 2 .... 3 ....

4.............................. 5.................................. 7..................................

THE SPANISH SPEAKING WORLD

The trade between Hispanic countries is increasing with each passing day. Billions of dollars have been invested by Indian companies in Latin America and Spain. India-Latin America trade relations account for more than $10 billion dollars annually and India –Spain amount to almost $6 billion as of 2011.

The name of some of the products is different in Spain and other Latin American countries. For example:

Spain	**Argentina**	**Mexico**	**English**
Frigorífico	Heladera	Refrigerador	Fridge
Nata	Crema de leche	Crema	Cream
Bocadillo	Sándwich	Torta/Sándwich	Sandwich
Plátano	Banana	Plátano	Banana
Piña	Ananá	Piña	Pineapple
Zumo	Jugo	Jugo	Juice
Guisante	Arveja	Chícharo	Pea
Vaquero	Jean	Jeans	Jeans
Falda	Pollera	Falda	Skirt
Sudadera	Buzo	Sudadera	Sweatshirt

CHAPTER

13 Looking for a job

ANUNCIO DE TRABAJO (A JOB ADVERTISEMENT):

EMPRESA MULTINACIONAL
con sede en Buenos Aires

BUSCA

DIRECTOR COMERCIAL
para su sucursal en Nueva Delhi.

- Edad entre 25 y 35 años
- Graduado en Administración de Empresas
- Conocimiento excelente de español e inglés.
- Experiencia profesional 0 - 2 años.
- Incorporación inmediata.

Interesados enviar C.V. a **tgbrecruitment@mail.ar**

A Curriculum Vitae (CV) is an essential tool to highlight your academic and professional qualifications. The CV may be followed by a personal interview. Shiv who finished M.B.A and is looking to change his job as the Manager of foreign trade in a company sees this advertisement.

Below is the Curriculum Vitae of Shiv which he sent to the Argentinean Company and he is now waiting for the interview call.

CURRÍCULUM VITAE

DATOS PERSONALES

Nombre:	Shiv Kumar Sharma
Fecha de nacimiento:	06/07/1986
Lugar de nacimiento:	Nueva Delhi
Nacionalidad:	Indio
Estado civil:	Soltero
Dirección:	B-235 Vasant Vihar, Nueva Delhi
Teléfono:	09438211443
Correo electrónico:	sksdelhi@gmail.com

FORMACIÓN ACADÉMICA

2010-2012:	Máster en Administración y Dirección de Empresas (M.B.A) por la Universidad Jamia Millia Islamia, Nueva Delhi.
2007- 2010:	Diplomatura en Comercio por la Universidad Jamia Millia Islamia, Nueva Delhi.

IDIOMAS

INGLÉS:	Nivel Alto
ESPAÑOL:	Nivel Alto (Diploma de Instituto Cervantes, Nueva Delhi)

INFORMÁTICA

Conocimiento amplio de Microsoft office, MS-DOS, Internet y Redes Sociales.

EXPERIENCIA PROFESIONAL

Septiembre de 2012 hasta el presente:	Gerente de comercio exterior en AMD Group, Nueva Delhi.

OTROS DATOS DE INTERÉS

- Voluntario en la ONG "I- Volunteers" en la que fui a los pueblos de Rajasthan para trabajar como auxiliar en el área de la salud femenina en el mes de junio de 2009.
- Tres años de experiencia teatral con el grupo IPTA, Delhi.

CURRICULUM VITAE

PERSONAL INFORMATION

Name:	Shiv Kumar Sharma
Date of birth:	06/07/1986
Place of birth:	New Delhi
Nationality:	Indian
Status:	Single
Address:	B-235 Vasant Vihar, New Delhi
Telephone:	09438211443
Email:	sksdelhi@gmail.com

ACADEMIC QUALIFICATIONS

2010-2012:	Master in Business Administration (MBA) from Jamia Millia Islamia University, New Delhi.
2007-2010:	Bachelor of Commerce from Jamia Millia Islamia University, New Delhi.

LANGUAGES

ENGLISH:	Advanced level.
SPANISH:	Advanced level. (Diploma from Instituto Cervantes, New Delhi)

COMPUTER KNOWLEDGE

Extensive knowledge of Microsoft Office, MS-DOS, Internet and Social Media.

PROFESSIONAL EXPERIENCE

September 2012 to present: Foreign Trade Manager in AMD Group, New Delhi.

OTHER DETAILS

- Volunteer at NGO "I-Volunteers" in which I went to the villages of Rajasthan in order to work as an assistant in the area of women's health in June 2009.
- Three years of theatre experience with the IPTA group, Delhi.

Dialogue:	Diálogo:
Rodrigo, an old friend of Shiv, sees him in a café and asks him about his job:	***Rodrigo, un viejo amigo de Shiv lo ve en un café y le pregunta de su trabajo:***
Rodrigo: Hello Shiv, how is work?	**Rodrigo:** Hola Shiv, ¿qué tal el trabajo?
Shiv: Everything is fine but I want to change now. I have applied for the job of Marketing Manager in an Argentinean company.	**Shiv:** Todo bien pero quiero cambiar ya. He solicitado el trabajo como Gerente de Marketing en una empresa argentina.
Rodrigo: Have they called you for the interview?	**Rodrigo:** ¿Te han llamado para la entrevista?
Shiv: No, not yet but today I have talked to the Secretary of the Managing Director and she has told me that I am one of the favorites for the post.	**Shiv:** No, todavía no pero hoy he hablado con la Secretaría del Director General y me ha dicho que soy uno de los favoritos para el puesto.
Rodrigo: Such a good news, Shiv! Good Luck with everything.	**Rodrigo:** ¡Qué buena noticia Shiv! Mucha suerte con todo.
Shiv: Thank you, Ruth.	**Shiv:** Gracias, Ruth.

Vocabulario	**Vocabulary**
La agencia de empleos	Placement agency
El presidente	President / Chairman
Consejero Delegado	Director General / CEO
El analista de inversiones	Financial analyst
El director de ventas	Sales manager
El economista	Economist
El gerente / director de recursos humanos	HR Manager
La empresa / compañía	Company
Los socios	Partners
La reunión	Meeting
La Sociedad Anónima	Public Limited Company
La Sociedad Limitada	Private Limited Company

Organización no gubernamental (ONG)	Non-Governmental Organisation (NGO)
La empresa multinacional	Multinational Company
El Máster en Administración de Empresas	MBA
El banco	Bank
El consultor / asesor	Consultant
La consultoría / asesoría	Consultancy
La acción	Share
El accionista	Shareholder
La bolsa	Stock market
El cheque	Cheque
El comercio internacional	International trade
El comercio doméstico	Domestic trade
La competencia	Competition
La carrera	Career
El hombre de negocios	Businessman
La mujer de negocios	Businesswoman

GRAMMAR

I. Present Perfect Tense.

In the dialogue above, you have been introduced to a new tense which is called present perfect or *pretérito perfecto*. This is used when we talk about recent past or past actions that continue to have some relation with the present. Below you will find some more usage of this particular tense.

Shiv *ha estudiado* en la Universidad Jamia Millia Islamia.	Shiv has studied in the Jamia Millia University.
Ha hecho teatro en su vida estudiantil.	He has done theatre in his student life.
También *ha trabajado* en una ONG.	He has also worked in an NGO.
Ha sido un estudiante muy inteligente.	He has been a very intelligent student.
Ha tenido una vida laboral muy buena hasta ahora.	He has had a very good professional life till now.

Present Perfect Tense is formed by the verb " haber" and the past participle. The past participle used in the perfect tense doesn't change.

	Haber	Past participle of the verb " Trabajar"	
(Yo)	he	trabajado	I have worked
(Tú)	has	trabajado	you have worked
(Ud, él, ella)	ha	trabajado	you, he , she have/has worked
(Nosotros)	hemos	trabajado	we have worked
(Vosotros)	habéis	trabajado	you all have worked
(Uds, ellos/as)	han	trabajado	you all, they have worked

In order to form the past participle of the verb in Spanish, drop the "ar" ending and add *ado*, and drop the "er" and "ir" endings and add *ido*.

Habl**ar** – habl**ado** (spoken)

Com**er** – com**ido** (eaten)

Viv**ir** – viv**ido** (lived)

Some verbs which have irregular past participles are given below:

Decir- dicho (said/ told)

Ver – visto (seen)

Hacer – hecho (done)

Escribir – escrito (written)

Poner – puesto (put)

Volver – vuelto (returned)

Examples:

He dicho la verdad.	I have told the truth.
¿ Has visto la carta?.	Have you seen the letter?.
Ella ha hecho la tarea.	She has done the work.
Hemos escrito el correo electrónico.	We have written the e-mail.
¿Habéis solicitado el puesto?	Have you all applied for the post?
Ellos han vuelto de Portugal.	They have returned from Portugal.

TASKS AND EXERCISES:

I. **As per the example given in the lesson, draft your own CV completing the following information:**

Datos personales:

Formación académica:

Idiomas:

Experiencia profesional:

Otros datos de interés:

II. **Below is an extract from the job interview taken by the Managing Director of The Green Box Company. Can you match the appropriate responses with the questions asked?**

1.	¿Me puede hablar algo de usted?	A.	Porque quiero trabajar en un ámbito internacional.
2.	¿Por qué quiere cambiar de empleo?	B.	Espero un promedio entre $ 25.000 y $ 30.000 al año.
3.	¿Ha tenido alguna experiencia en ventas?	C.	Me he graduado en Administración de Empresas por la Universidad Jamia Millia Islamia y también hablo español muy bien.
4.	¿Por qué quiere trabajar en nuestra empresa?	D.	Sí, Trabajo como gerente comercial y tengo mucha experiencia en esta área.
5.	¿Cuánto espera ganar?	E.	Porque es una empresa multinacional muy conocida.

III. **Today Pepa, who works as a secretary, had to do a lot of work before leaving the office. She has managed to do some but she has not been able to complete all of the work. In the fragment below, fill in the verbs to ascertain what Pepa has and has not done today:**

Antes de salir Pepa................ (preparar) el informe pero no .... (redactar) la carta al Director de Ventas.

.... (llamar) a los socios para la reunión de mañana pero no..................(decir) a su jefe la hora de la reunión.

Pepa................(colocar) el archivo para la reunión de mañana en el archivador pero se ....(olvidar) anotar el nombre y el número del mismo.

..................(hacer) casi todo pero no le..............(decir) a su jefe que ella no va a venir mañana.

THE SPANISH SPEAKING WORLD

Los indignados movement and Spanish economic crisis.

Los indignados movement, also referred to as 15- M movement in Spain, has its roots in the economic crisis which Spain is going through since last few years. It is a series of protests which started on 15th May 2011 against the government with people demanding an end to political corruption and anti-people economic policies.

Puerta del Sol, the central square of Madrid became the centre point of the protest and los indignados movement became an inspiration for other "occupy" movements like those that happened in London and in New York Central Park.

CHAPTER

14 Writing letters and e-mails

Writing letters and e-mails in a foreign language requires a set of skills. It is through letters, e-mails and nowadays, internet chats, that people in the world communicate and interact. Below you will find examples of formal and informal letters and e-mails in Spanish which contain the basic features of letter writing in Spanish.

1. Una carta informal

Nueva Delhi, 4 de agosto de 2012

Querida María:

¿Qué tal estás? ¿Cómo están Pedro y los niños? Acabo de regresar de España. Fuimos por un mes para pasar las vacaciones de verano. España es un país precioso. Viajamos mucho. Fuimos a las playas y vimos los monumentos y catedrales preciosos. Me gustó mucho el sur de España donde hay mucha influencia árabe en la arquitectura y en el arte. La Alhambra en Granada me pareció un paraíso. Viajamos en tren y en autobuses y recorrimos casi todo el país desde el norte hasta el sur. En total, la experiencia fue inolvidable.

Un abrazo

Swati

An informal letter

New Delhi, August 4, 2012

Dear Maria,

How are you? How are Peter and the children? I just got back from Spain. We went for a month to spend the summer holidays. Spain is a beautiful country. We travelled a lot. We went to the beaches and saw beautiful monuments and cathedrals. I really liked the south of Spain where there is a lot of Arab influence in art and architecture. The Alhambra in Granada seemed a paradise. We traveled by train and bus and toured most of the country from north to south. Overall, the experience was memorable.

Hugs

Swati

As you can note, the informal letters that people write to their friends and families are more free style and don´t follow very specific format. But there are some things that you should always take into consideration:

- **The date and place format:** The date and place are always written on the upper right hand side corner and follow a specific format. First the name of the place is written followed by a comma and then the date in the format **.....de .... de......** (date, month, year).
- **Addressing the receiver:** In informal letters it is common to begin with **querido/a** or **hola** followed by the name of the person.

  For eg: Querida Maria: *Dear Maria,*

Note the colon after the name instead of the usual coma in English.

- **The body:** The body of the letter can comprise of anything. It is more free style.
- **The closing of the letter:** The informal letters close with any of the following expressions:

Un abrazo	Hugs
Un fuerte abrazo	A strong hug
Un beso	Kisses
Un beso grande	A big kiss

Besos	Kisses
Un saludo	Regards
Un afectuoso saludo desde Delhi	Warm regards from Delhi
Con cariño	With love

2. **Escribir un correo electrónico** **Writing an E-mail**

Below is a model of an informal e-mail which we generally send to our friends or acquaintances:

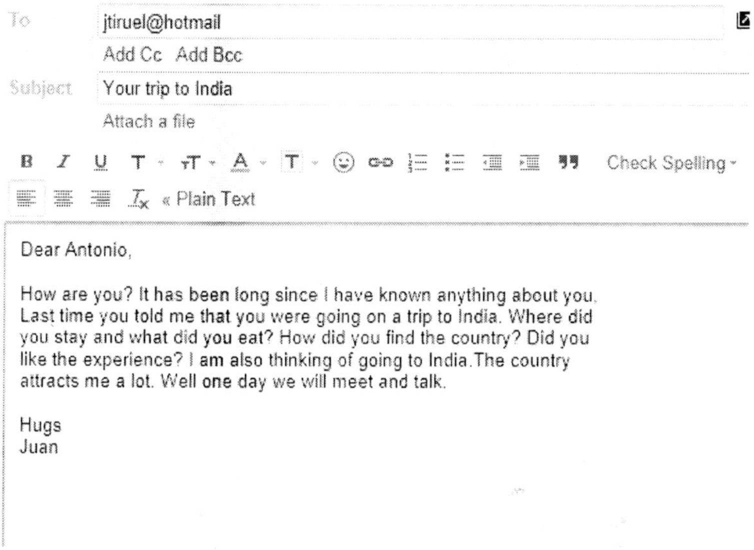

To jtiruel@hotmail

Add Cc Add Bcc

Subject Your trip to India

Attach a file

B I U T TT A T Check Spelling

« Plain Text

Dear Antonio,

How are you? It has been long since I have known anything about you. Last time you told me that you were going on a trip to India. Where did you stay and what did you eat? How did you find the country? Did you like the experience? I am also thinking of going to India.The country attracts me a lot. Well one day we will meet and talk.

Hugs
Juan

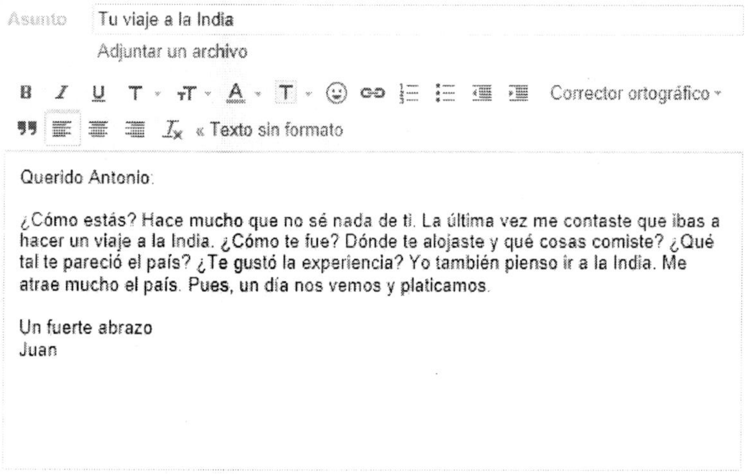

Asunto Tu viaje a la India

Adjuntar un archivo

B I U T TT A T Corrector ortográfico

« Texto sin formato

Querido Antonio:

¿Cómo estás? Hace mucho que no sé nada de ti. La última vez me contaste que ibas a hacer un viaje a la India. ¿Cómo te fue? Dónde te alojaste y qué cosas comiste? ¿Qué tal te pareció el país? ¿Te gustó la experiencia? Yo también pienso ir a la India. Me atrae mucho el país. Pues, un día nos vemos y platicamos.

Un fuerte abrazo
Juan

3. Una carta formal (A formal letter)

12 de junio de 2012

ABC Agencia de Viajes

C/ Gibraltar, 8

28023 Madrid

Estimado Sr. Rodríguez:

Por la presente le comunico que en el mes de julio mi familia y yo fuimos a México. Salimos el día 6 de julio y regresamos el 28. Hicimos una reserva en un hotel a través de su agencia. Tuvimos muchos problemas a lo largo de nuestra estancia. El hotel no **era** bueno y aunque el desayuno **estaba** incluido en el pago, nos avisaron que no y tuvimos que pagar otra vez. Cuando salimos del hotel, los porteros ni nos llevaron las maletas hasta el taxi. El servicio **era** muy malo y por eso queremos una devolución del dinero que pagamos.

Quedo en espera de su respuesta.

Un cordial saludo,

Juan Gómez Rodríguez

June 12, 2012

ABC Agencia de Viajes
8, Gibraltar street
Madrid 28023

Dear Mr. Rodriguez:

This is to inform you that in the month of July my family and I went to Mexico. We left on July 6 and returned on 28th. We made a reservation in a hotel through your agency. We had many problems throughout our stay. The hotel was not good and even though the breakfast was included in the payment, they told us that it was not and we had to pay again. When we were leaving the hotel, the porters didn´t even carry the suitcases till the taxi. The service was very bad and so we want a return of the money that we paid.

Awaiting your response,

Yours sincerely,
Juan Gómez Rodríguez

While writing a formal letter one has to be careful with regard to the format. A general letter starts with the date on the upper right hand side corner and then if the letter is not written on a letter head (*membrete)* then the sender writes his or her name and address followed by the name and address of the receiver. Note the way the Spanish address format is written.

XYZ S.A (S.A is *Sociedad Anónima* which means Public limited company.)

C/ Princesa (C/ is the short form of *Calle* which means street)

28040 Madrid (The zip code is written before the name of the city)

Generally there is no subject line in a Spanish formal letter.

Greetings: When we don't know the name of the person we are addressing then we start with *Muy señor mío* , *Muy señora mía, Muy señores míos* or *Estimado/a/os/as Señor/a/es/as* and if we know the name of the addressee then it is a simple *Estimado señor Rodríguez, Estimada Sra. Pérez.*

When you know the addressee well then you can address them as *Estimado/ Estimada* followed by the name. Or a simple *Querido/Querida* followed by the name is also appropriate.

Body: The body of the letter can start with:	
El motivo de la presente.............	The purpose of the letter is......
Tengo el gusto de ponerme en contacto con usted..	I have the pleasure to get in touch with you.
Por la presente le comunico.......	This is to inform you...
Closing: The closing can have varied styles:	
En espera de sus noticias.	Waiting for your reply
Atentamente	Yours sincerely
Un cordial saludo	Regards
Le saluda atentamente	Yours truly

VOCABULARY

La carta	Letter
La dirección	Address
El correo electrónico	E-mail
¿Cuál es su correo electrónico?	What is your e-mail?
El remitente	Sender
El recipiente	Receiver
El asunto	Subject
El sobre	Envelop
La tarjeta postal	Postcard
El telegrama	Telegram
El membrete	Letterhead
La firma	Signature
Signos	**Sign**
@	arroba
_	guión bajo
/	barra diagonal
.	punto
,	coma

GRAMMAR

The **informal letters** above and the **e-mail** are talking about something which happened during a specific moment in the past (i.e. a trip that they took). They are narrating the incidences or events that happened during that period. This tense is used for telling the action which finished in the past (the verbs which is highlighted in the informal letter). For example, in English we use definite past for one time action: *I saw Maria yesterday, I bought a new dress.*

In the **formal letter**, a new tense has been highlighted in bold and it is called the imperfect tense or past continuous tense. It is used to talk about past repeated actions, description of some place or some people. It tells about something that used to happen or was happening during a particular time period in the past.

Form:

First let's see how these two verb forms are conjugated.

I. El pretérito indefinido (The definite past)

There are two types of endings in the preterit tense. One is for –**ar** ending verbs and the second one is for –**er** and –**ir** ending verbs.

For the -AR verbs, add the following endings: -é, **aste, ó, amos, asteis, aron.**

Hablar (to speak)

(yo)	hablé	I spoke
(tú)	hablaste	you spoke
(él/ella/usted)	habló	he/she/you spoke
(nosotros/as)	hablamos	we spoke
(vosotros/as)	hablasteis	you spoke
(ellos/ellas/usted)	hablaron	they/you spoke

Example:

Hablé con mi madre ayer. I spoke with my mother yesterday.

For the –ER and - IR verbs, add the following endings: **-í, iste, ió, imos, isteis, ieron.**

	Comer	**Vivir**
(yo)	comí	viví
(tú)	comiste	viviste
(él/ella/usted)	comió	vivió
(nosotros/as)	comimos	vivimos
(vosotros/as)	comisteis	vivisteis
(ellos/ellas/usted)	comieron	vivieron

Example:

Ella no comió nada. — She didn't eat anything.

Mi abuelo vivió desde 1929 hasta 1991. — My grandfather lived from 1929 to 1991.

Note: Remember that a written accent is very important in Spanish. Only a written accent sometimes differentiates between present tense and definite past. For example, *hablo* is I speak and *habló* is he spoke.

The irregular verbs:

There are many verbs which are irregular in pretérito indefinido. Some of them are given below.

	Dar (to give)	Hacer (to do)	Tener (to have)	Ir (to go)
(yo)	di	hice	tuve	fui
(tú)	diste	hiciste	tuviste	fuiste
(él/ella/usted)	dio	hizo	tuvo	fue
(nosotros/as)	dimos	hicimos	tuvimos	fuimos
(vosotros/as)	disteis	hicisteis	tuvisteis	fuisteis
(ellos/ellas/usted)	dieron	hicieron	tuvieron	fueron

Examples:

Le di una carta. — I gave him a letter.

Ella hizo la tarea. — She did the work.

Tuve la oportunidad de irme — I had the opportunity to leave.

Ellos fueron a casa. — They went home.

II. El pretérito imperfecto (Past continuous)

There are two types of endings in the imperfecto. One is for –**ar** ending verbs and the second one is for –**er** and –**ir** ending verbs.

For the -AR verbs, add the following endings: **-aba, abas, aba,** ábamos**, abais, aban.**

habl<u>ar</u> (to speak)

(yo)	hablaba	I used to speak/ I was speaking
(tú)	hablabas	you used to speak/ you were speaking
(él/ella/usted)	hablaba	he/she/it/you used to speak
		he/she/it was speaking, you were speaking
(nosotros/as)	hablábamos	we used to speak/ we were speaking
(vosotros/as)	hablabais	you used to speak/ you were speaking
(ellos/ellas/usted)	hablaban	they/you used to speak
		they/you were speaking

Example:

Ella hablaba inglés. She was speaking English.

For the –ER and - IR verbs, add the following endings: **- ía, ías, ía, íamos, íais, ían.**

	Com<u>er</u>	**Viv<u>ir</u>**
(yo)	comía	vivía
(tú)	comías	vivías
(él/ella/usted)	comía	vivía
(nosotros/as)	comíamos	vivíamos
(vosotros/as)	comíais	vivías
(ellos/ellas/usted)	comían	vivían

Examples:

De vez en cuando, ellos comían en mi casa.	Occasionally, they used to eat at my home.
Antes yo vivía en un pueblo.	Before I used to live in a village

The irregular verbs:

There are only three irregular verbs in imperfecto. They are *Ser, Ver* and *Ir.*

	Ser	Ver	Ir
(yo)	era	veía	iba
(tú)	eras	veías	ibas
(él/ella/usted)	era	veía	iba
(nosotros/as)	éramos	veíamos	íbamos
(vosotros/as)	erais	veíais	ibais
(ellos/ellas/usted)	eran	veían	iban

Examples:

Mi amigo era muy inteligente. — My friend was very intelligent.

Cuando yo era niño, veía mucho la televisión. — When I was a child, I used to watch lot of TV.

Todos los días ellos iban a la escuela. — Every day they used to go to the school.

III. Use of indefinido and imperfecto tenses

Indefinido	Imperfecto
1. It is used for past actions that ended at a concrete moment or at a precise time. *Ayer compré un recuerdo para él.* Yesterday I bought a souvenir for him. *El tren para Barcelona salió a las ocho.* The train for Barcelona left at 8 o clock.	1. Actions that used to happen regularly in the past. *Todos los días yo iba al templo.* Every day I used to go to the temple.
2. Actions which had a beginning and a known end. *De mayo a septiembre estuve de vacaciones.* From May till September I was on vacation	2. Describing places and persons in the past. *Había mucha gente en el hotel.* There were many people in the hotel. *El paisaje era muy hermoso.* The landscape was very beautiful.

3. Sequence of actions happening at a particular moment. *Fui al baño, me duché, me vestí y salí del hotel.* I went to the bathroom, I took a shower, I got dressed up and then I left the hotel	3. Describing continuous actions in the past. *Manolo iba a la playa y nadaba en el mar.* Manolo used to go to the beech and swim in the sea.
4. Describing actions which took place when something else was happening. The sudden action will be in indefinido. *Caminaba por la playa cuando alguien me llamó.* I was walking on the beach when somebody called me.	

TASKS AND EXERCISES

I. Write a letter to your friend describing what you did yesterday on the basis of the pictures given below?

Ejemplo:

Ayer por la mañana me levanté a las 7. — Yesterday morning I got up at 7.

1. Por la mañana

(ducharse)

(preparar el desayuno)

2. Por la tarde

(ir al Mercado)

3. Por la noche

(cenar con la familia)

(ver la televisión antes de dormir)

II. Ana is writing a letter to her friend describing her experience in Barcelona. Fill in the blanks to complete the letter.

Madrid, 2 de mayo de 2012

Querida amiga:

Ayer regresé de Barcelona. Yo....................(ir) allí por dos días. Me ....(alojar) en un hostal. El primer día....................(salir) del hostal a las 8 de la mañana para ir a Montserrat. ....(pasar) dos horas allí y ....(volver) por la noche. Estaba muy cansada por eso ....(acostarse) muy temprano.

El día siguiente no ....(hacer) mucho. Sólo ....(pasear) por las Ramblas. En Barcelona yo..................................(divertirse) bastante. Es una ciudad preciosa.

Nos vemos pronto

Un beso

Ana

III. See the pictures and complete the below sentences telling what happened at that particular moment using the following:

mi novia me llamó, alguien tocó el timbre, vi al gato, tuvimos un accidente, el ladrón entró por la ventana

1. Iba al Mercado cuando ....

2. Viajábamos en autobús cuando ....

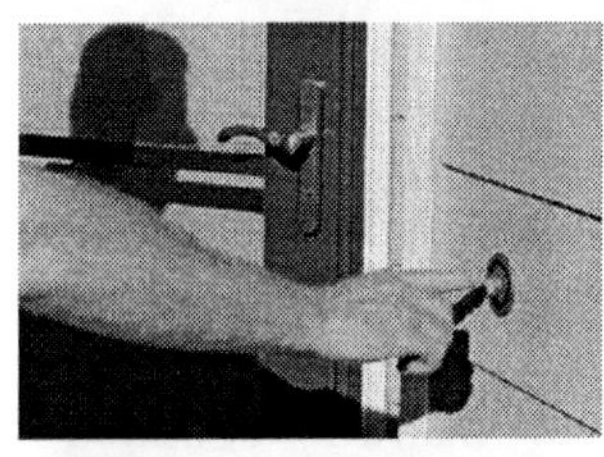

3. Me duchaba cuando ....

4. Dormía en casa cuando ....

5. Leía el periódico cuando ....

IV. Your father and you have lived in different times. In his youth, he used to do something that you don't do now. Likewise you do somethings now that your father didn't do in his younger days.

Compare the changes that have happened with the change of time.

Ejemplo: Hablar por teléfono fijo. Hablar por móvil

Antes mi padre hablaba por teléfono fijo pero **ahora** yo hablo por móvil.

	Tu Padre		**Tú**
1.	Escuchar la radio	1.	Escuchar el iPod
2.	Escribir cartas	2.	Escribir correo electrónico
3.	Viajar en autobús	3.	Viajar en metro
4.	Ir al teatro	4.	Ir al concierto de rock
5.	Leer periódicos	5.	Leer noticias en internet

THE SPANISH SPEAKING WORLD

Hispanics in United States

Hispanics in US constitute a major chunk of the total ethnic population in the United States. They are the people with origins in Hispanic America or the Iberian Peninsula. Presently they constitute more than 16 % of United States' population and now command a greater political and economic influence. Most of the Hispanics are either of Mexican, Cuban or Puerto Rican origin and have Spanish as their mother tongue. The intermingling of Hispanics with the rest of US population has given rise to a curious mix of language called *Spanglish* which is now being spoken by various young people in Hispanic localities. *Spanglish* is not a pidgin language but a totally informal language with no fix set of rules. It has also been used in the Chicano literature for the reaffirmation of cultural identities by the Hispanic people.

CHAPTER 15 Making plans

Do you make New Year resolutions? Do you fulfill them? We don´t know about you but Iñakí is a boy who makes New Year resolutions each year and fulfills them. For the year 2013, he has the following plan:

¿Haces buenos propósitos del año nuevo? ¿Los cumples? No sabemos de ti pero Iñaki es un chico que cada año hace buenos propósitos del año nuevo y los cumple. Para el año 2013 tiene el siguiente plan:

En 2013 me despertaré temprano.	In 2013, I will wake up early.
Nunca faltaré las clases.	I will not bunk clases.
Dejaré de fumar.	I will quit smoking.
Dedicaré más tiempo a mi familia.	I will give more time to my family.
Ayudaré a mi madre en los quehaceres del hogar.	I will help my mother in the household chores.
Conseguiré un trabajo.	I will get a job.
Aprenderé a tocar la guitarra.	I will learn to play guitar.

Can you notice the new verb form that has appeared in the text above? Since Iñaki is talking about the future, the verbs are all conjugated in the future tense. Below are some more situations where we use this construction.

Dialogue:	**Diálogo:**
La casa de Beatriz:	***Beatriz's house***
Beatriz's new house is in the countryside. Rumana comes to visit and starts chatting	*La nueva casa de Beatriz está en el campo. Rumana viene de visita y empieza a charlar.*
Rumana: How big the house is! How many bedrooms does it have?	**Rumana:** ¡Qué grande es la casa! ¿Cuántos dormitorios tiene?
Beatriz: There are four bedrooms and three bathrooms. We also have a tennis court behind and a garden in the front.	**Beatriz:** Hay cuatro dormitorios y tres cuartos de baño. También tenemos una pista de tenis detrás y un jardín en frente.
Rumana: Are you going to live here always or will you come here occasionally?	**Rumana:** ¿Vas a vivir aquí siempre o vendrás de vez en cuando?
Beatriz: No, I will not live here.We will only spend the summer and rest of the time, we will be in our apartment in the city.	**Beatriz:** No, no voy a vivir aquí. Sólo pasaremos el verano y el resto de tiempo estaremos en nuestro piso de la ciudad.
Rumana: As the house is empty, are you thinking of buying the furniture here or will you bring it from the city?	**Rumana:** Como la casa está vacía, ¿piensas comprar los muebles de aquí o los traerás de la ciudad?
Beatriz: I think I am going to buy everything here.	**Beatriz:** Creo que voy a comprar todo aquí.
Rumana: Well, in that case, I am giving you my cousin's number. He has a furniture store. If I tell him, he will also give you a discount.	**Rumana:** Pues, en este caso, te doy el número de mi primo. Tiene un almacén de muebles. Si le digo, también te hará un descuento.
Beatriz: How nice you are Rumana! Thanks a lot.	**Beatriz:** ¡Qué amable eres Rumana! Muchas gracias.
Rumana: You are welcome.	**Rumana:** De nada.

VOCABULARY

La casa	House
La habitación/ El cuarto	Room
El cuarto de baño	Bathroom
La sala de estar	Living room
El comedor	Dinning room
La dirección	Address
Mi dirección es.......	My address is.......
El timbre	Doorbell
La cocina	Kitchen
La terraza	Terrace
El edificio	Building
El piso	Flat
El apartamento	Apartment
La planta baja	Ground floor (Planta means floor in non residential buildings)
El primer piso	First floor (Piso means apartment and also floor in residential buildings)
Vivo en el primer piso.	I live on the first floor.
El segundo piso	Second floor
El tercer piso	Third floor
El balcón	Balcony
El jardín	Garden
La llave	Key
El frigorífico/la nevera	Fridge
El ventilador	Fan
La lavadora	Washing machine
La puerta	Door
La ventana	Window
La cortina	Curtain
La alfombra	Carpet
La salida	Exit

La salida de emergencia	Emergency exit
La entrada principal	Main entrance
La escalera	Stairs
El trastero	Storage room

GRAMMAR

I. The Future Tense:

The future tense is used to talk about something which is going to happen or will happen in the future.

1. **The most common way of saying something in future is by using the verb *Ir a +infinitive (to be going to do something)* which you have already studied in lesson 6.**

For example:

La próxima semana voy a trabajar mucho.	Next week I am going to work a lot.
Ana va a dormir.	Ana is going to sleep.
Ellos van a ver la película.	They are going to see the movie.

2. **For an intended action and plan, we use *pensar +infinitive* (to think / to intend)**

¿Qué piensas hacer este fin de semana?	What are you thinking of doing this weekend?
Voy a lavar la ropa.	I am going to wash the clothes.

3. **Otherwise, we use future tense in Spanish. The table given below shows the future tense of the regular verbs.**

Hablar (to speak)

(yo)	hablaré	I will speak
(tú)	hablarás	You will speak
(él, ella, usted)	hablará	He/she/you will speak
(nosotros/as)	hablaremos	We will speak
(vosotros/as)	hablaréis	You will speak
(ellos, ellas, ustedes)	hablarán	They/you will speak

Example:

Hablaré con él. I will speak to him.

Comer (to eat)

(yo)	comeré	I will eat
(tú)	comerás	You will eat
(él, ella, usted)	comerá	He/she/you will eat
(nosotros/as)	comeremos	We will eat
(vosotros/as)	comeréis	You will eat
(ellos, ellas, ustedes)	comerán	They/you will eat

Example:

Comeremos en casa. We will eat at home.

Escribir (to write)

(yo)	escribiré	I will write
(tú)	escribirás	You will write
(él, ella, usted)	escribirá	He/she/you will write
(nosotros/as)	escribiremos	We will write
(vosotros/as)	escribiréis	You will write
(ellos, ellas, ustedes)	escribirán	They/you will write

Example:

Escribiré una carta mañana. I will write a letter tomorrow.

Irregular verbs in the future tense

There are few irregular verbs in the future tense, it is to say, that they do not follow the above mentioned pattern.

Hacer (to do)	Decir (to say)	Salir (to leave)	Tener (to have)	Venir (to come)
haré	diré	saldré	tendré	vendré
harás	dirás	saldrás	tendrás	vendrás
hará	dirá	saldrá	tendrá	vendrá
haremos	diremos	saldremos	tendremos	vendremos
haréis	diréis	saldréis	tendréis	vendréis
harán	dirán	saldrán	tendrán	vendrán

Example:

Lo haré luego. I will do it later.

¿Qué dirá mi madre? What will my mother say?

Saldremos mañana. We will leave tomorrow.

Yo tendré la oportunidad. I will have the opportunity.

¿Vendrás a la oficina mañana? Will you come to the office tomorrow?

Poder (can, to be able to)	Saber (to know)	Poner (to put)	Querer (to want)
podré	sabré	pondré	querré
podrás	sabrás	pondrás	querrás
podrá	sabrá	pondrá	querrá
podremos	sabremos	pondremos	querremos
podréis	sabréis	pondréis	querréis
podrán	sabrán	pondrán	querrán

Example:

Ella no podrá bailar. She will not be able to dance.

Ustedes sabrán todo mañana. You all will know everything tomorrow.

Lo pondré aquí. I will put it here.

¿Qué querrás hacer? What will you want to do?

TASKS AND EXERCISES

I. Rashmi goes to meet a fortune teller (el adivino). Fill in the blank using future tense.

Rashmi: Señor, quiero saber cómo ....(ser) mi futuro. ¿Con quién ....(casarse, yo)? ¿......(tener, yo) buen trabajo?

Adivino: Bueno Rashmi, ...(trabajar) en una empresa multinacional. El próximo año ....(viajar) al extranjero. Pero como lo veo, tú ....(tener) un poco de dificultad en encontrar el hombre de tu vida.

Rashmi: ¡No me asuste señor! Qué pasará? Cómo lo ....(encontrar, yo)?

Adivino: Él..............(estar) cerca de ti siempre pero no lo .... (reconocer, tú) y por fin me parece que ....(casarse, tú) con otro hombre.

Rashmi: ¡Qué triste estoy!

Adivino: No pasa nada hija. Tu marido te ....(hacer) muy feliz y ....(tener, vosotros) mucho dinero y un chalet en Marbella.

II. Form the future of the sentences given below with Ir a + infinitive.

Yo te envío un correo / Mañana	**Mañana te voy a enviar un correo.**

a. Compramos una casa en Nueva Delhi / El mes que viene.

b. Él vive en un pueblo/ El año que viene.

c. Os digo la verdad / Esta noche.

d. Tengo dos hijos / En el futuro

THE SPANISH SPEAKING WORLD

Spanish is one of the world's most learnt language and in India, too, the teaching and learning of Spanish has achieved a lot of importance, mostly because of the growing ties with the Latin American world and also because of the global outsourcing of consumer services to India. Spanish is taught in various centres across India. Universities like Jawaharlal Nehru University, Delhi University, English and Foreign Languages University, Doon University have graduate programmes in Spanish. Universities like Jamia Millia Islamia and Mumbai University are offering Certificate, Diploma and Advanced Diploma courses in Spanish. Other than this, various universities and management institutes offer part time or optional Spanish courses. Instituto Cervantes in New Delhi is the official Spanish language institute of the Government of Spain. Apart from this, Spanish is also taught in various other private institutes in many big cities as well as in the embassies of some of the Latin American countries. For a detailed list of institutes offering Spanish courses please visit:

http://www.jnu.ac.in/Faculty/rsaxena/RESOURCES/univ_courses.htm

Keys to Exercise

LESSON 1

B- 1262-MJ - be - uno, dos, seis, dos - eme, jota

M-8092-PF – eme – ocho, zero, nueve, dos – pe, efe

Z-6259-TL – zeta – seis, dos, cinco, nueve – te, ele

SE-6359-T – ese, e – seis, tres, cinco, nueve - te

BI-4179-SO – be, i – cuatro, uno, siete, nueve – ese, o

SS-4159-MK – ese, ese – cuatro, uno, cinco, nueve – eme, ka

B-6309-LT – be – seis, tres, zero, nueve – ele, te

M-2747-OC – eme – dos, siete, cuatro, siete – o, ce

LESSON 2

I. A. días, está, bien.

B. tal, muy, tú.

C. noches, hasta

D. adiós, fin de

II. A. buenos días.

B. hasta el lunes

C. hasta pronto/luego

D. ¡que te vaya bien!

III. A. informal

B. formal

C. formal

D. informal

E. informal

LESSON 3

II. Me llamo Arun Kumar. Apellido. Sí, soy indio. En la empresa IBM. Es 8824576801

III.

(Yo)	hablo	trabajo	escribo	me llamo	soy
(Tú)	hablas	trabajas	escribes	te llamas	eres
(Ud, él, ella)	habla	trabaja	escribe	se llama	es
(Nosotros)	hablamos	trabajamos	escribimos	nos llamamos	somos
(Vosotros)	habláis	trabajáis	escribís	os llamáis	sois
(Uds,ellos/as)	hablan	trabajan	escriben	se llaman	son

LESSON 4

I. 1. soy, somos. 2. está.
3. hay.

II. 1. es. 2. están.
3. hay. 4. está.
5. sois. 6. hay

III. agricultor, cantante, donante, estudiante, gerente, periodista, piloto, taxista.

Y	N	J	Q	D	S	Y	D	Y	P	E	M	J	P	N
G	K	C	C	P	K	L	J	O	B	S	I	W	I	U
A	G	R	I	C	U	L	T	O	R	T	J	B	L	Z
V	O	S	O	U	O	C	I	W	O	U	V	J	O	G
C	C	X	W	E	Z	E	V	B	A	D	N	V	T	X
W	W	R	Q	V	T	O	K	G	Q	I	Q	T	O	X
X	J	V	J	N	U	N	R	L	T	A	Q	G	E	P
C	G	G	E	R	E	N	T	E	A	N	T	S	T	U
A	F	R	E	R	C	Z	V	I	M	T	E	T	N	J
N	E	N	U	U	A	T	S	I	D	E	I	R	E	P
T	B	W	L	Z	L	I	D	O	N	A	N	T	E	V
A	Y	T	A	X	I	S	T	A	R	J	T	E	E	Z
N	O	U	E	O	I	W	S	B	T	B	A	S	W	M
T	Y	Q	L	U	Z	N	Y	D	S	L	A	I	E	C
E	Y	P	K	A	P	E	R	I	O	D	I	S	T	A

LESSON 5

I. tengo, llama, está, son, son, hija

II. 1. abuelo. 2. suegra. 3. sobrino. 4. hijo. 5. prima

III. 1. su. 2. sus. 3. nuestra. 4. mi. 5. tú

IV. esta, esta, esa, aquella

LESSON 6

I. 1. son las ocho.
2. son las tres.
3. es la una y veinte.
4. son las doce en punto.
5. son las seis menos cuarto.

III. 1. desde, hasta.
2. al.
3. con. .
4. de, a

LESSON 7

I. 1. lavarse.
2. levantarse.
3. ir.
4. desayunar.
5. afeitarse.
6. ducharse.
7. salir.
8. acostarse.
9. volver.
10. despertarse

II. 1. Manolo se afeita.
2. Javier se ducha.
3. El bebé duerme.
4. Sebastián se lava la cara.

III. 1. D. 2. E. 3. B. 4. A. 5. C

LESSON 8

I. Swati baila de vez en cuando, Prabhat ve la televisión cada noche, Dinesh esquia una vez al año, Rohan corre cada mañana, Shivani va al cine a menudo.

Note: All the adverbs of frequency given in the question can be used in these situations depending on what you want to say.

II.
1. gusta.
2. gustan.
3. duelen.
4. encanta.
5. interesa

III.
1. ¿Te gusta vivir en la India?
2. A mis padres no les gusta navegar por la red.
3. Me gusta jugar al fútbol.
4. En mi tiempo libre, me gusta leer las novelas.
5. A Carlos le gustan los chocolates.

LESSON 9

I.
1. hace viento.
2. hace sol.
3. está nublado.
4. llueve.

II.
1. hace sol.
2. llueve.
3. está despejado.
4. hay.
5. calor

III.
1. mucho.
2. poco, muy.
3. muy.
4. mucha.
5. Mucho.

IV. abril, agosto, enero, invierno, marzo, mayo, primavera, verano.

V.	M	Q	V	V	E	N	E	R	O	Y	I	M	K	N
K	Z	O	E	F	R	N	U	O	Y	A	A	X	N	F
O	P	N	P	R	I	M	A	V	E	R	A	L	C	O
C	Ñ	N	E	E	A	R	M	Z	K	B	E	J	Y	E
I	C	O	I	K	D	N	O	E	S	N	V	P	V	D
A	Q	V	T	R	A	G	O	S	T	O	A	O	E	U
B	N	A	G	O	S	T	O	L	Q	C	M	F	R	V
R	D	A	G	Q	H	D	M	I	A	L	I	R	A	A
I	U	M	B	F	H	X	A	J	G	Z	R	D	N	N
L	S	F	H	G	W	V	Y	F	X	G	P	R	O	X
E	W	E	Q	K	Z	G	O	V	D	V	X	I	Q	O
E	I	T	I	N	V	I	E	R	N	O	E	S	O	H
O	O	M	T	M	J	I	R	H	C	R	F	F	Y	Z
E	K	U	B	D	J	O	Z	T	R	O	L	I	A	J
P	L	C	V	E	M	A	R	Z	O	W	J	I	M	N

LESSON 10

I. 1. D. 2. E.
3. F. 4. B.
5. C. 6. A.

II. **i.** A. a la izquierda.
B. debajo de la mesa.
C. sobre/encime de la mesa.
D. a la derecha.
E. sobre/encime de la mesa.

ii. A. No, está cerca.
B. No, está a la derecha del sofá.
C. No, está a la izquierda de la mesa.
D. Sí.
E. Sí.

III. 1. ¿Cuánto cuesta este bolso?
2. ¿Cuánto cuesta una botella del vino?

3. ¿Cuánto cuestan estos zapatos?
4. ¿Cuánto cuestan las gafas del sol?

LESSON 11

I. Hola, ¿qué desea comer?.

De primero quiero una ensalada mixta.

¿Y de segundo que desea?

De segundo pollo con champiñones.

¿Y algo de beber?

Pues, me trae una botella de vino por favor.

Muy bien ¿Desea algo de postre?

Sí, una tarta de queso.

Enseguida.

II. les, nos, nos, os, me.

III. para, por, por, por, para.

LESSON 12

I.
1. quiero comprar una camisa negra.
2. ¿ qué talla de camisa lleva?.
3. la roja.
4. ¿me la puedo probar?
5. con tarjeta

II.
1. corbata.
2. falda.
3. camiseta.
4. guantes.
5. sombrero.
6. bufanda.

LESSON 13

II. 1. C. 2. A. 3. D. 4. E. 5.B.

III. ha preparado, ha redactado, ha llamado, ha dicho, ha colocado, ha olvidado, ha hecho, ha dicho.

LESSON 14

I.

Nueva Delhi, 4 de noviembre de 2012

Querida Ana:

¿Qué tal estás?. Te cuento lo que hice ayer. Por la mañana me levanté a las 7. Me duché y preparé el desayuno. Luego, por la tarde fui al mercado para hacer las compras. Por la noche, cené con la familia. Vi la televisión antes de dormir. Eso es todo lo que hice ayer.

Un abrazo

Anil

II. fui, alojé, salí, pasé,volví, me acosté, hice, paseé, me divertí.

III.
1. vi al gato.
2. tuvimos un accidente.
3. alguien tocó el timbre.
4. el ladrón entró por la ventana.
5. mi novia me llamó.

IV.
1. Antes escuchaba la radio pero ahora yo escucho el iPod.
2. Antes escribía cartas pero ahora escribo correo electrónico.
3. Antes viajaba en autobús pero ahora viajo en metro.
4. Antes iba al teatro pero ahora voy al concierto de rock.
5. Antes leía periódicos pero ahora leo noticias en internet.

LESSON 15

I. será, me casaré, tendré, trabajarás, viajarás, tendrás, encontraré, estará, reconocerás, te casarás, hará, tendréis.

II.
1. El mes que viene vamos a comprar una casa en Nueva Delhi.
2. El año que viene él va a vivir en un pueblo.
3. Esta noche os voy a decir la verdad.
4. En el futuro voy a tener dos hijos.

Additional Vocabulary

COUNTRIES AND NATIONALITIES

Países	Countries	Nacionalidades	Nationalities
Inglaterra	England	inglés (masc)	English
		inglesa (fem)	
Francia	France	francés (masc)	French
		francesa (fem)	
Alemania	Germany	alemán (masc)	German
		alemana (fem)	
España	Spain	español (masc)	Spanish
		española (fem)	
Portugal	Portugal	portugués (masc)	Portuguese
		portuguesa (fem)	
Italia	Italy	italiano (masc)	Italian
		italiana (fem)	
Holanda	Holland	holandés (masc)	Dutch
		holandesa (fem)	
Turquía	Turkey	turco (masc)	Turkish
		turca (fem)	
Grecia	Greece	griego (masc)	Greek
		griega (fem)	
Argentina	Argentina	argentino (masc)	Argentinian
		argentina (fem)	
Estados Unidos	United States	estadounidense	American
México	Mexico	mexicano (masc)	Mexican
		mexicana (fem)	
Brasil	Brazil	brasileño (masc)	Brazilian
		brasileña (fem)	
Cuba	Cuba	cubano (masc)	Cuban
		cubana (fem)	

Venezuela	Venezuela	venezolano (masc)	Venezuelan
		venezolana (fem)	
Canadá	Canada	canadiense	Canadian
India	India	indio (masc)	Indian
		india (fem)	
China	China	chino (masc)	Chinese
		china (fem)	
Japón	Japan	japonés (masc)	Japanese
		japonesa (fem)	
Pakistán	Pakistan	pakistaní	Pakistani
Australia	Australia	australiano (masc)	Australian
		australiana (fem)	
Rusia	Russia	ruso (masc)	Russian
		rusa (fem)	

FOOD AND DRINKS

El pan	Bread
Los huevos	Eggs
La mantequilla	Butter
El queso	Cheese
El yogur	Yoghurt
La carne	Meat
El pollo	Chicken
El pescado	Fish
El marisco	Seafood
La carne de cerdo	Pork
El arroz	Rice
La tarta	Cake
El chocolate	Chocolate
La sal	Salt
El azúcar	Sugar
El helado	Ice cream

La ensalada	Salad
La comida rápida	Fast food
La hamburguesa	Burger
Las patatas fritas	French fries
La pizza	Pizza
El agua	Water
El agua mineral	Mineral water
El zumo	Juice
El zumo de naranja	Orange juice
El zumo de manzana	Apple juice
El té	Tea
El café	Coffee
La máquina de café	Coffee machine
La cerveza	Beer
El vino	Wine
El cóctel	Cocktail
La leche	Milk
FRUITS	
Las uvas	Grapes
La manzana	Apple
El plátano	Banana
La naranja	Orange
La fresa	Strawberry
El mango	Mango
La papaya	Papaya
La sandía	Watermelon
El melocotón	Peach
La guayaba	Guava
La piña	Pineapple
La pera	Pear
La cereza	Cherry

TRANSPORT	
El coche	Car
La moto	Motorcycle
La bicicleta	Bicycle
El tranvía	Tram
El metro	Metro
El avión	Aeroplane
El autobús	Bus
El tren	Train
El andén	Platform
El número de andén	Platform number
El barco	Ship
El taxi	Taxi
El horario	Timetable
La salida de emergencia	Emergency exit
La máquina de rayos x	X-ray machine
El tráfico	Traffic
El semáforo	Traffic light
El paso elevado	Flyover
La estación de autobuses	Bus station
La parada de autobús	Bus stop
El cinturón de seguridad	Seat belt
La gasolina	Petrol
El diesel	Diesel
El accidente de coche	Car accident
El seguro	Insurance
La avería	Breakdown

BANK	
El banco	Bank
El mostrador	Counter
El cajero	Cashier

El cliente	Customer
La firma	Signature
El pago	Payment
La cuenta corriente	Current account
La cuenta de ahorros	Savings account
La comisión bancaria	Bank commission
La transferencia bancaria	Bank transfer
La inversión	Investment
El director de banco	Bank manager
El número de cuenta	Account number
El cajero automático	ATM machine
El pin	Pin number
La tarjeta de crédito	Credit card
El billete	Note
La moneda	Currency
El préstamo	Loan
El tipo de interés	Interest rate
ELECTRONIC GADGETS	
La radio	Radio
La televisión	Television
El teléfono fijo	Telephone (Landline)
El teléfono móvil	Mobile phone
La computadora/ El ordenador	Computer
El ordenador portátil/ El portátil	Laptop
La calculadora	Calculator
El fax	Fax
La impresora	Printer
El micrófono	Microphone
El telegrama	Telegram
La cámara digital	Digital camera
La cámara de videos	Video Camera

El reloj	Watch
El secador de pelo	Hair dryer
El webcam	Webcam
El mando a distancia	Remote control
El lector de MP3	MP3 player
El video juego	Video game
COMPUTER	
El ordenador	Computer
El ordenador portátil	Laptop
El servidor	Server
El RAM	RAM
La CPU	Central processing unit
La memoria	Memory
La red	Network
El disco duro	Hard disc
El hardware	Hardware
El teclado	Keyboard
El ratón	Mouse
La pantalla	Screen
El altavoz	Speaker
La carpeta	Folder
El fichero	File
El fondo	Wallpaper
La barra de menú	Menubar
En línea	On-line
El documento adjunto	Attachment
El correo electrónico	Email
El programa	Program

LEISURE	
El cine	Cinema hall
La película	Movie
La película romántica	Romantic movie
El teatro	Theatre
La entrada	Ticket
La flauta	Flute
El violín	Violin
El concierto	Concert
La guitarra	Guitar
La canción	Song
El museo	Museum
El monumento	Monument
El parque nacional	National park
El parque de atracciones	Theme park
El casino	Casino
La visita con guía	Guided tour
La oficina de información	Information office
El ciclismo	Cycling
El senderismo	Hiking
El picnic	Picnic
La playa	Beach
El bikini	Bikini
El bañador	Swimsuit
El camping	Camping
SHOPPING	
El centro comercial	Shopping centre
El ascensor	Lift
El perfume	Perfume
Los desodorantes	Deodorants

Los aseos	Toilets
La ropa de caballero	Men´s wear
La ropa de señora	Women´s wear
Los aparatos eléctricos	Electrical godos
Las ofertas	Offers
Las rebajas	Sale
El servicio al cliente	Customer services
Los probadores	Changing romos
El dependiente	Sales assistant
La caja de bombones	Box of chocolates

CITY

La ciudad	City
El colegio	School
La universidad	University
El templo	Temple
La mezquita	Mosque
La iglesia	Church
La calle	Street
La tienda	Shop
El edificio	Building
El aparcamiento	Parking
La zona peatonal	Pedestrian zone
La zona industrial	Industrial area
La señal de tráfico	Traffic light
La oficina	Office
El rascacielos	Skyscraper
El puente	Bridge

MEDIA	
La prensa	Press
El canal	Channel
Las noticias	News
En directo	Live
El entrevistador	Interviewer
La entrevista	Interview
La presentadora de las noticias	Newsreader
La cámara	Camera
El cámara	Cameraman
El micrófono	Microphone
El concurso	Game show
La telenovela	Soap
La radio	Radio
La estación de radio	Radio station